LIFE OF THE TRAIL 1 HISTORIC HIKES IN
EASTERN BANFF NATIONAL PARK

LIFE OF THE TRAIL 1 HISTORIC HIKES IN
EASTERN BANFF NATIONAL PARK

By Emerson Sanford & Janice Sanford Beck

Rocky
Mountain Books
VANCOUVER • VICTORIA • CALGARY

Rocky Mountain Books
#108 – 17665 66A Avenue
Surrey, BC V3S 2A7
www.rmbooks.com

Rocky Mountain Books
PO Box 468
Custer, WA
98240-0468

Library and Archives Canada Cataloguing in Publication

Sanford, Emerson
    Historic hikes in eastern Banff National Park / Emerson Sanford, Janice Sanford Beck.

(Life of the trail 1)
Includes bibliographical references and index.
ISBN 978-1-894765-99-2

    1. Hiking—Alberta—Banff National Park—Guidebooks. 2. Banff National Park (Alta.)—Guidebooks. I. Beck, Janice Sanford, 1975- II. Title. III. Series.
GV199.44.C22A443 2008   796.51097123'32   C2007-907284-4

Library of Congress Control Number: 2007943169

Edited by Meaghan Craven
Proofread by Joe Wilderson
Book and cover design by Chyla Cardinal
Front cover photo by Emerson Sanford
Back cover photo courtesy of the Whyte Museum of the Canadian Rockies Archives (V701/LC-313)
All interior images supplied by the authors except as otherwise noted

Printed and bound in Hong Kong

Rocky Mountain Books gratefully acknowledges the financial support of the Government of Canada through the Book Publishing Industry Development Program (BPIDP); the Canada Council for the Arts; and the province of British Columbia through the British Columbia Arts Council and the Book Publishing Tax Credit for our publishing activities.

This book has been produced on 100% post-consumer recycled paper, processed chlorine free and printed with vegetable-based dyes.

The Rocky Mountains are precious and sacred to us. We knew every trail and mountain pass in this area. We had special ceremonial and religious areas in the mountains. In the olden days some of the neighbouring tribes called us "People of the Shining Mountains." These mountains are our temples, our sanctuaries, and our resting places. They are a place of hope, a place of vision, a place of refuge, a very special and holy place, where the great spirit speaks to us. Therefore, these mountains are our sacred places.

—Chief John Snow, *These Mountains Are Our Sacred Places*[1]

Contents

ACKNOWLEDGEMENTS

The preparation for a book of this type requires the perusal of many secondary sources; during our research we read hundreds of books. The authors of the books we used are acknowledged in the Notes section at the end of this book. Many of the books are still in print and readily available. Others required much diligence on the part of reference librarians to obtain interlibrary loans, and we wish to thank the personnel at the Canmore Public Library, especially Michelle Preston and Hélène Lafontaine, for their assistance. Other books and documents were available only through the Whyte Museum & Archives, and we appreciate the efforts of Lena Goon, Elizabeth Kundert-Cameron, D.L. Cameron, Don Bourdon, and Lisa Christensen for steering us on the right track and obtaining materials and images for us.

The Alpine Club of Canada in Canmore kindly allowed us the use of their collection of the *Canadian Alpine Journal*. Others who provided useful discussion and/or materials during the course of the research were: W. John Kosh; Herb Ratsch of Brightest Pebble Publishing; Ron Tozer, Algonquin Park archivist; David Peyto of Peyto Lake Books; Scott Jevons, GIS Specialist, Government of Alberta; and Rod Wallace and Don Mickle of the National Parks Warden Service. Thanks also to Madam Justice Wailan Low, literary executor, for permission to reprint a portion of Earle Birney's "Bushed."

A large part of the effort in preparing these volumes was in hiking all of the trails and routes described in the history section. Emerson wishes to thank his wife, Cheryl, for the many hours that she spent taking him to trailheads and picking him up several days later at a different location, sometimes on remote gravel roads that were not easily accessible. In addition, Cheryl always had in hand a copy of the itinerary for the hike in order to contact the Warden Service if the solo hiker did not emerge from the wilderness at the appointed time (he always did).

In addition, Emerson wishes to acknowledge the many hikers on remote backcountry trails who stopped to chat and made the solitary hikes more enjoyable. Many of these people are mentioned in the text. Those hikers who are not mentioned were on trails near Lake Minnewanka, Athabasca Pass, Wildflower Creek valley, the Jasper Park North and South Boundary, Job Pass, the Rockwall, and undoubtedly others. There were also several wardens along the way who contributed to the author's enjoyment of the backcountry experience.

For Janice, this project has been a labour of love, squeezed in amongst various family, community, and work responsibilities. She would like to thank her partner, Shawn, and children, Rowan and Christopher, for their willingness to accommodate the time required for a project of this magnitude. She would also like to thank her parents for sharing their love of history and introducing her to the trails these volumes bring to life.

Finally, the authors would like to express their appreciation to Don Gorman, Meaghan Craven, Chyla Cardinal, and others at Rocky Mountain Books for their efforts in bringing this work from manuscript to publication.

INTRODUCTION

From the Canadian Rockies' original inhabitants to twenty-first century enthusiasts, those who venture into the heart of these mountains encounter a place of deep significance. The lofty peaks and enchanted valleys represent temples, sanctuaries, and resting places to many modern adventurers, just as they did to Chief John Snow's people. Over the past two centuries of non-Aboriginal presence, the Rockies have also represented a challenging barrier to overcome, a treasure trove of scientific data, and a site for respite and recreation.

The history of exploration in the Canadian Rocky Mountains south of the Peace River district can be divided into four distinct periods. The first consists of the years prior to the arrival of non-Aboriginal peoples. Archaeological evidence indicates that indigenous peoples have been present in parts of today's Banff National Park for at least 10,500 years. The various peoples occupying the plains and mountains appear to have traded extensively; many of the well-developed trails through the mountains are believed to have been trade routes. But because Native travels through the Rockies were not recorded, very little is known of this early phase of travel and exploration.

The second period of Rocky Mountain exploration was dominated by early nineteenth-century fur-trade explorers searching for a passage to the Pacific coast. Most were accompanied by Native or Métis guides whose forebears had been navigating the trails for centuries. There was very little exploration in the mountains during this period; the explorers' main concern was simply to get through safely.

The third period of exploration runs from the 1858 Palliser expedition to the completion of the Canadian Pacific Railway in 1885. Hoping to promote settlement and defend the territory against American expansion, the Canadian government sent surveyors and scientists to gain as much information as possible about the West. Mountain travel focused on finding a route for the railway through the Rockies and the Selkirks. Ironically, while most trails used during this period followed Aboriginal routes, the CPR's selected route through Kicking Horse and Rogers passes (which subsequently also became the route of the Trans-Canada Highway) was not a favoured Native route.

Completion of the railway ushered in the fourth period, that of the tourist/explorers and mountaineers. These intrepid individuals explored the mountains for the sheer pleasure of it. Some were motivated by the thrill of discovery; some basked in the solitude of the wilderness. Others were driven to hunt mountain goats, sheep, and grizzlies, and to climb mountains – especially the myriad yet-unscaled peaks. This period, from the end of the nineteenth century through to the Great Depression, could also be called the era of the pack train, as most trips were guided by outfitters.

It was undoubtedly the outfitters and guides of this fourth period of exploration who had the greatest impact on establishing today's alpine trail system. Guides such as Tom Wilson, Jim Simpson, and Bill Peyto were the real trail-makers, not the wealthy mountaineers and explorers who hired them. On top of their daily duties of rounding up horses, cooking breakfast, breaking camp, and packing the horses, guides were also responsible for route finding, especially when no trails existed. Through their efforts to overcome obstacles such as forest fires, burnt over areas (brulés), and muskeg, the number of identifiable trails multiplied. As these trails became more heavily used, camping spots with pasture for horses and a supply of wood and water were set up at intervals approximately one day apart. Often the campsites had neatly stacked supplies of tepee poles.[2] Anyone found to have destroyed tepee poles – by burning them as firewood, for instance – was blacklisted by the entire outfitting community.

Despite the work of the outfitters, most exploration of this fourth period is credited to the well-to-do visitors such as J. Norman Collie and Walter Wilcox, who hired the outfitters. In fact, these men likely had very little to do with the route finding that led to the discovery of previously unexplored valleys and mountain passes. Their names are attached to many of the historic routes in this book only because they instigated the trips and identified the areas they wanted to explore. The Coleman brothers, Arthur and Lucius, are a notable exception to this trend; they outfitted themselves and shared the work on the trail, doing most of the route finding themselves.

In 1909 a development took place in Rocky Mountains Park (now Banff National Park) that would significantly impact trails throughout the Rocky Mountains: Fire and Game Guardians were hired to enforce park regulations.[3] Up until this time, CPR employees had cut some recreational trails near the railway and timber cullers cut others. With the formation of the Guardian Service in 1909, park officials decided to create a network of trails to facilitate the enforcement of park regulations. Trails were usually constructed by contractors following existing trails or routes previously blazed by the Warden Service. By 1912 Park Superintendent Howard Douglas reported the employment of five permanent wardens at Rocky Mountains Park "who patrol all portions of the park on regular trails."[4] By 1914 the Warden Service reported that some sixty separate trails existed in Rocky Mountains Park and that all were being regularly patrolled.

By 1920 the Fire and Game Guardian Service had evolved into the Warden Service. At this point, the fourteen hundred miles (22,526 kilometres) of trails in the park[5] included both those leading to scenic vistas and those used primarily for fire and game protection. Most wardens considered it a matter of pride to know their territory intimately. In addition to patrolling identified trails, they would explore side valleys, often making their own trails. At least some of the non-historic trails likely originated in this way.

As trails became better established and more people visited the mountains, another form of backcountry travel emerged: the escorted outfitted trip. These trips were organized by a leader who recruited guests to participate. The two most famous examples of such leaders are Pennsylvanian Caroline Hinman, who, beginning in 1917, brought groups of teenaged girls to the mountains for outings of up to several weeks; and John Murray Gibbon, a Canadian Pacific Railway publicist, who established the Trail Riders of the Canadian Rockies and their organized group excursions in 1923. Similar types of tours include A.O. Wheeler's walking tours to Mount Assiniboine and trips organized by the Skyline Trail Hikers of the Canadian Rockies.

In the 1920s automobile use greatly increased the number of visitors to the national parks. However, few explored the longer trails and more distant areas unless accompanied by guides licensed to operate in the parks. In 1925 Curly Phillips lamented: "The day of the pack train is pretty well over, as the tourist of today wants speed and the only way to get it is where there is good roads and motor cars...We have wonderful country here and I have spent 17 years building up an outfit and a business only to find when I got to the top that there was nothing there and no possible future to the business."[6]

By the mid 1930s the advent of packsacks with steel frames, lightweight tents and sleeping bags, and Primus stoves meant that individuals could carry all they needed to survive for two weeks in the wilderness without need for pack trains or guides. By the time these modern-day backpackers started following the now well-established trails into the backcountry, the day of the pack train was indeed over. Very few new trails have been established since the beginning of the 1930s, and of those most are simply realignments or replacements of existing trails for environmental reasons.

For the purpose of the volumes in *Life of the Trail*, the historic routes through the Rockies have been divided into regions based on the geographical boundaries that influenced nineteenth-century travellers. Modern-day boundaries are ignored. This first volume in the series discusses historic routes and hikes in the area bounded by the North Saskatchewan River on the north and the Mistaya River, Bow River, and Lake Minnewanka on the west and south.

Howse Pass, the earliest fur-trade route across the Rockies, is described in *Life of the Trail 2*, which presents the area bounded by the Kicking Horse River to the south; the Columbia Icefield to the north; and the Bow, Mistaya, and North Saskatchewan rivers to the east. Later explorers created a popular return trip from the Kootenay Plains by adding the old Native trail down the Amiskwi River to the Howse Pass route. Also included in this volume are the Yoho Valley and the Castleguard Meadows. Today this area is bounded by the Trans-Canada Highway to the south and the Icefields Parkway to the east.

Routes within each volume are discussed in order of first use. The most historically significant trip described in this volume is David Thompson's journey along the Red Deer River to meet the Kootenays and take them back to Rocky Mountain House. Later, the Native route over Pipestone Pass to the Kootenay Plains was used extensively by tourist/explorers and mountaineers. Today this area is bounded by the David Thompson Highway (#11) in the north and the Icefields Parkway (#93), the Bow Valley Parkway (#1A) and Lake Minnewanka on the west and south.

Each volume, designed to fit neatly into a pack, outlines the history of these routes, giving the modern-day traveller a feel for how they were established and who has used the trails since. With a little imagination, the reader can envision Caroline Hinman at the head of a string of thirty horses, escorting a group of teenaged girls through the mountains. You can share in David Thompson's enthusiasm as he catches his first glimpse of the Rockies and Martin Nordegg's excitement as he accompanies his daughter along a trail so central to his working life. And you can join A.P. Coleman in his delight in "renewing our acquaintance with mountain trails, those capricious, tantalising, exasperating, and yet wholly seductive pathways, leading through bogs and fallen timber nowhere, and yet opening out the sublime things of the world and giving many an unforeseen glimpse of Nature hard at work constructing a world."[7]

Moreover, you can retrace their journeys yourself.

During the 1990s, the authors hiked many of these trails together. Since then, Emerson has re-hiked each and every one of them to ensure the most accurate trail information possible. When we use the first person "I" in the book regarding adventures along the trails, we are referring to Emerson and his experiences. We provide a complete trail guide for the modern traveller, including trails that do not fall within park boundaries. We provide elevation graphs to assist the hiker in estimating the effort required to cross each mountain pass, and we have highlighted trails on a topographic map.

To complete the stories, we offer general descriptions of the trails, highlight the scenic wonders to be encountered, and describe interesting incidents we have experienced during our adventures along the routes. We hope that through these narratives, hikers and armchair travellers alike will join the Reverend George M. Grant in sympathizing "... with the enthusiast, who returned home after years of absence, and when asked what he had as an equivalent for so much lost time,– answered: 'I have seen the Rocky Mountains.'"[8]

Spruce grouse frequently seen along the trails in the Rocky Mountains are often referred to as "fool hens" because they do not fear humans. This trait made for many an easy meal in the early days.

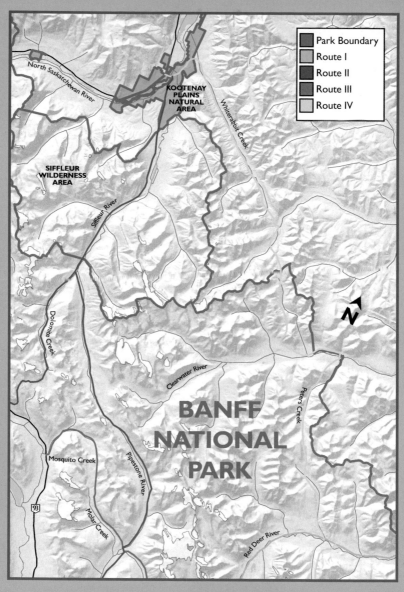

■	Park Boundary
■	Route I
■	Route II
■	Route III
□	Route IV

North Saskatchewan River

KOOTENAY
PLAINS
NATURAL
AREA

Whiterabbit Creek

SIFFLEUR
WILDERNESS
AREA

Siffleur River

Dolomite Creek

Clearwater River

Peters Creek

BANFF

NATIONAL

PARK

Mosquito Creek

Pipestone River

93

Molar Creek

Red Deer River

The Northern Portion of the Front Ranges
from the Red Deer River to the North
Saskatchewan River

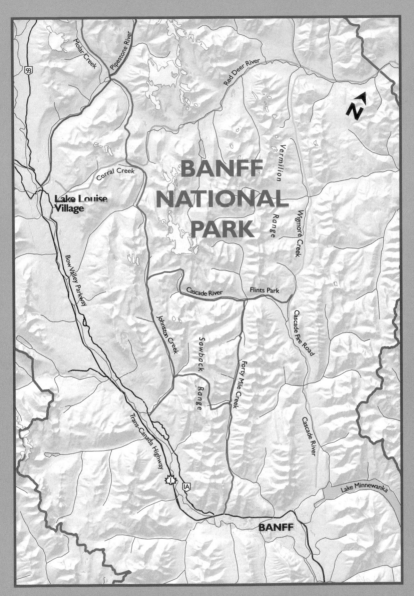

The Southern Portion of the Front Ranges
from Lake Minnewanka to the Red Deer River

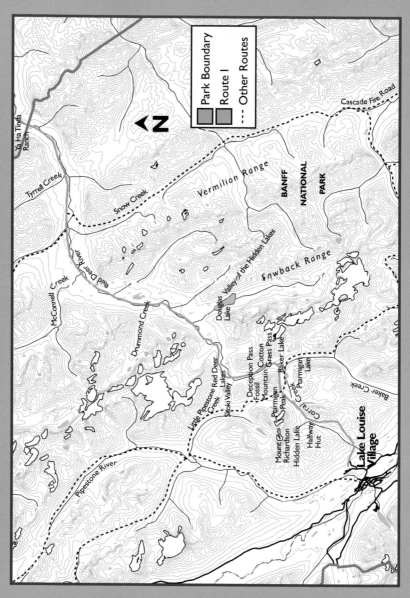

Route I from Lake Louise to the Ya Ha Tinda Ranch
along Corral Creek and the Red Deer River

ROUTE I

*Behold the Shining Mountains: The Kootenay and David Thompson Route
from Ya Ha Tinda Ranch to the Bow River*

Hiking through the Ya Ha Tinda Ranch in July 2002, I spotted a team
of mules approaching on the old wagon road (Cascade Fire Road).
The team stopped and the driver greeted me with a pleasant smile and
genuine hello. The amiable backcountry gentleman informed me that
he was on his way to pick up supplies and a cook for Melcher's Ranch,
located on a strip of land between the Ya Ha Tinda Ranch property and
the boundary of Banff National Park. Though it was early in the season
and he was alone at the ranch, he informed me that he had – as was his
custom – left two Thermoses of freshly brewed coffee with mugs, sugar,
and whitener on the front deck of the main ranch house for any visitors
who might come along. He encouraged me to stop on my way through,
telling me that I would be met by a pack of five or six friendly dogs.
The dogs were friendly, and the coffee was excellent. My faith in the
goodness of humanity was bolstered.

CHRONOLOGY

1800 David Thompson travels west along the Red Deer River to the Red Deer Lakes to meet a band of Kootenays coming from the west. This is the first record of Europeans entering the Rocky Mountains south of the Peace River area.

Thompson sends two traders, Charles La Gasse and Pierre Le Blanc, back across the mountains with the Kootenay band. This is the first record of Europeans crossing the mountains.

1884 Dr. George Mercer Dawson travels along the Red Deer River to the Red Deer Lakes, then along the Little Pipestone Creek and Pipestone River to the Bow Valley.

1895 Walter Wilcox and Bill Peyto travel through the Skoki and Ptarmigan valleys as part of a trip along the Sawback Range.

1904 Walter Wilcox walks into the Ptarmigan Valley from Lake Louise. Later that year, Billy Warren escorts Mary Schäffer and friends on a week-long trip to Ptarmigan Valley.

1905 Schäffer and friends travel over Boulder Pass and along the Red Deer River.

1906 A.O. Wheeler and assistants survey the Ptarmigan Valley area.

1909 Dr. Charles Walcott travels to the Ptarmigan Valley with his son, Stewart.

J.W.A. Hickson enters the valley intent on climbing but is turned back by bad weather. He returns the following year, reaches the head of the Red Deer Lakes, and climbs Mount Douglas.

1910 Carl Rungius becomes the first artist to venture into the Ptarmigan Valley.

1911 James Foster Porter and eleven mountaineering friends thoroughly explore the area from Merlin Meadows to the Pulsatilla valley, naming many of the features, including the Skoki Valley.

1912   Carl Rungius returns to the Ptarmigan Valley.

1914   The Warden Service cuts a trail into the Ptarmigan Valley.

1915   The Alpine Club of Canada holds its annual camp at Phacelia (Hidden) Lake.

1916   Dr. Walcott returns with Mary Vaux Walcott and sets up camp at the same spot he had used in 1909.

1917   Caroline Hinman's first Off the Beaten Track tour in the Canadian Rockies concludes by travelling along the Red Deer River from Snow Creek to its headwaters, then on to the Ptarmigan Valley and Lake Louise.

1921   Walter Wilcox pushes beyond the Red Deer Lakes to explore Douglas Lake and the Valley of Hidden Lakes.

The Walcotts make their way up Baker Creek and camp in the Wildflower Creek valley.

1922   The Walcotts have their men cut a trail to Douglas Lake, no doubt along Wilcox's old trail.

1923   The Walcotts camp near Baker Lake.

1924   The Walcotts return to both Baker Lake and the Wildflower camp at the head of Baker Creek. Later that summer they proceed along the Red Deer River to east of the Ya Ha Tinda Ranch.

1925   The Walcotts return to the Ptarmigan Valley. This is Charles Walcott's last trip to the Canadian Rockies.

1926   Lars Haukaness begins painting in the Ptarmigan Lake region.

1927   Caroline Hinman reverses her 1917 trip, proceeding from Lake Louise through the Ptarmigan Valley and along the Red Deer River to Snow Creek.

1929   Lars Haukaness suffers a fatal heart attack while returning from a painting trip to Ptarmigan Lake.

History

Natives and Fur Traders

With the following passage from the diary of fur trader David Thompson, recorded history of the second period of exploration in the Canadian Rocky Mountains south of the Peace River district began:

> October 14 [1800] Tuesday A very fine Day. At 7 ½ Am I set off for the Mountains with three Men, our Guide and several Pekenow Indians, who came with us from Hopes of Plunder. ... We went on about West 22 Miles [thirty-five kilometres] to the Foot of the high Cliffs, where at 2 ½ Pm we met the Kootanae Chief attended by about 26 Men and 7 Women. ... Our road today has been mostly along small Brooks – the sources of the Red Deer River – which every where intersect the Hills. ... [W]e again crossed & recrossed (the Brook), as we did the one before, until we gained the heights of the Mountain – where we found the road dry, very Hilly & stony. ... When we arrived on the Heights of the Mountains, at the Foot of those high Craigs that brave the storm in all it[s] Force, I wished to climb them to gain a View of the back Country, but they were inaccessible to human Feet, and the Care of the Kootanaes called for all my Time & Attention.[1]

Prior to the fur trade, Aboriginal peoples had travelled extensively through the mountains for thousands of years, exploring every valley and pass. Archaeologists have located forty-eight prehistoric sites in what is today Banff National Park.[2] In the Bow Valley, they have found butchering camps, flint-knapping sites, and diagnostic points ranging from the valley floor near the Vermilion Lakes to an alpine hunting camp on Corral Creek below Boulder Pass. Along the upper Red Deer River, they have located pit houses built by the Shuswap people approximately three thousand years ago.[3] One site, which contained eleven pit houses, showed a clear pattern of use over a period of sixteen hundred years, beginning twenty-nine hundred years ago. At the Ya Ha Tinda, a shallow basin along the Red Deer River just outside the park, forty-nine prehistoric sites have been located, indicating that prehistoric groups inhabited the valley for many winters, probably because it was a wintering range for bison.[4]

Other fur traders and trappers may also have entered this portion of the Rockies prior to David Thompson's adventures in 1800 but left no written record. By 1793 Alexander Mackenzie had followed rivers and trails far to the north to cross the mountains to the Pacific Ocean.[5] Others had certainly seen the mountains from a distance; most history texts credit Hudson's Bay Company (HBC) trader Anthony Henday with being the first European man to see the Rocky Mountains, in October 1754. Yet, although the phrase "Behold the Shining Mountains" is often attributed to Henday, he makes no obvious reference to a mountain range in his journal, and some conclude that it is unlikely he actually saw the Rocky Mountains.[6]

David Thompson himself spent the winter of 1787–88 with five other Hudson's Bay Company traders and the Peigans at their winter camp near the junction of the Bow and Kananaskis rivers. The traders had seen the Rocky Mountains in November, on their way to the camp.[7] Five years later, Peter Fidler, a Hudson's Bay Company explorer, surveyor, and map maker, and fellow HBC employee John Ward, travelled south along the foothills with a group of Peigan and Sarcee. They too saw the mountains in November 1792.[8] Yet neither Thompson nor Fidler nor their companions actually entered the mountains on these trips.

In 1799 both the Hudson's Bay Company and the North West Company (NWC) built forts on the northwest bank of the North Saskatchewan, just above the mouth of the Clearwater River. Although Acton House (HBC) and Rocky Mountain House (NWC) were built in the midst of Peigan territory, both companies hoped to attract the trade of the Kootenay people from west of the Rocky Mountains. The North West Company traders soon realized that this trade was unlikely to materialize, as the Kootenays were unwilling to risk their lives at the hands of the Peigans by coming to the fort. Following their usual policy, the NWC resolved to take their trade to the Kootenays, using Rocky Mountain House as a staging point.

It was for this reason that David Thompson – having switched allegiances from the HBC to the NWC – and his young wife, Charlotte, arrived at the fort at Rocky Mountain House in September 1800. Here Thompson was to meet Duncan McGillivray, his senior officer, who was designated to lead the company's expedition across the mountains. By early October, however, Thompson had heard news of a band of Kootenays approaching to trade at the fort. McGillivray was overdue, and Thompson was very anxious to meet with the Natives, both to gain information about their routes and to trade. On October 5, 1800, he set out south along the foothills toward the Red Deer River where he hoped to meet with the Kootenay band.

DAVID THOMPSON (1770–1857)

Known by the Natives of the Flathead Valley as Koo-Koo-Sint ("the man who looks at stars"), David Thompson was an astronomer, ardent naturalist, and talented storyteller. First and foremost, however, he was a surveyor – the greatest pioneering geographer in North America. He was born in London of Welsh parents. His father died when he was only two years old, leaving his mother to raise him and a newborn son on her own. Unable to support her family, she placed David in a charity school, Gray Coat School at Westminster, London, at the age of seven. Seven years later, in 1784, he was apprenticed to the Hudson's Bay Company and sent to Churchill on Hudson Bay, where he began work as a clerk. A year later he was sent to York Factory, 150 miles (241 kilometres) to the south, and soon after was sent inland. The following winter, he travelled far to the southwest, wintering with a band of Peigans in what is now southern Alberta.

In December 1788 Thompson accidentally broke his leg while hauling a loaded sled. During his lengthy recovery, he was fortunate to spend the winter of 1789–90 with the Hudson's Bay Company's resident surveyor, Philip Turner, who taught him the basics of surveying and gave him an old Dollond sextant. From then on Thompson took measurements wherever he went, gradually filling in the empty spaces on his map of western North America.

In the spring of 1797, Thompson left the Hudson's Bay Company – presumably because of their lack of interest in exploration and surveying. He joined the North West Company, where he began fifteen years of productive work. He was not really interested in a career of trading furs; rather, he was motivated by a burning desire to survey the country. The Nor'westers, as his new colleagues were known, were much more interested in exploring, hoping that it might lead to future financial gain.

Thompson's first assignment was to survey the new boundary between the United States and the British territories. He undertook the task at a hectic pace, completing the survey in only ten months. By 1800, the company was preparing for a push over the mountains into the lucrative fur-trading areas of what are today Washington and Oregon. As part of that westward movement, David Thompson was sent to Rocky Mountain House, where our story begins. He went on to pioneer fur-trade routes over Howse and Athabasca passes and to survey the Columbia River from source to mouth, one of his greatest accomplishments.

David Thompson retired from the fur trade altogether in 1812, arriving in Montreal in the fall of that year. With him was his wife, Charlotte, a Métis woman he had married in 1799 when she was just fourteen. Charlotte's mother was Cree; her father, Patrick Small, a North West Company partner. In one draft of his *Narrative*, Thompson wrote: "My lovely wife is of the blood of these people, speaking their language, and well educated in the English language, which gives me a great advantage."[9] They

Artist's rendition of what David Thompson
may have looked like while surveying.

bought a house in Terrebonne, Quebec, where they settled with
their five children. According to D'Arcy Jenish, Thompson had
his wife and five children baptised in Montreal in 1912. The
children ranged in age from eleven years to eighteen months.
They had thirteen altogether, the last born in 1829.

Thompson retired with significant savings accumulated over his years in the fur trade, but a series of bad investments and poor loans soon depleted his funds. He spent the first twenty months after his retirement completing his ten-foot-long map of the Northwest, then worked at a variety of jobs, mainly surveying, trying to make ends meet. He died in poverty on February 10, 1857, at the age of eighty-six.

There is no known portrait of David Thompson, but J.J. Bigsby gives a striking verbal picture: "He was plainly dressed, quiet and observant. His figure was short and compact, and his black hair was worn long all around, and cut square, as if by one stroke of the shears, just above the eyebrows. His complexion was of the gardener's ruddy brown, while the expression of deeply furrowed features was friendly and intelligent, but his cut-short nose gave him an odd look."[10]

October 5th [1800] Sunday A fine cloudy Day. At 8 Am the Men crossed the River [Clearwater], La Gasse, Beauchamp, Morrin, Pierre Daniel, Boulard & myself, with the He Dog, a Cree, and the Old Bear, a Pekenow Indian, our Guide. We had an assortment of Goods, amounting to about 300 Skins, & each of us a light Horse, belonging to himself, and 3 Horses of the Company's to carry the Baggage. ... [W]e went on about ... 2 ½ M to the parting of the Roads, where finding we had forgot to take a Kettle with us, I sent La Gasse back again to the House for one. Mean Time we went on ... 10 ½ M to the Brook Bridge: here we put up to wait La Gasse, who came in the Evening with 2 Kettles. Fine weather.[11]

Thompson's party first saw the Rocky Mountains the following day, while travelling along the Red Deer River near the present-day town of Sundre:

> October 6th, [1800] Monday In the Morn Cloudy, with a small shower of Rain – afterwards fine. At 6 am set off – ...SSW 2M to the Red Deer River, which we crossed – we then went on up along the River, mostly on the Gravel Banks ... and went on thro' a tolerable fine Plain SW 2M to a bold Brook.... Here we had a grand view of the Rocky Mountains, forming a concave segment of a Circle.... All its snowy cliffs to the Southward were bright with the Beams of the Sun, while the most northern were darkened by a Tempest.[12]

By October 13 the party had reached an area known to the Stoney people as "Wahpay Pah Tinda," or "Prairie in the Mountains,"[13] the site of present-day Ya Ha Tinda Ranch. This is where today's trail through the mountains along the Red Deer River begins.

Thompson explained that "From the top of a very high knoll, I had a very extensive View of the Country: from the southward extending by the westward to the North, it was every where Ranges of woody Hills lying nearly parallel to the Mountain, and rising one behind another higher and higher to the snowy Summits of the Mountain."[14] The next day, the North West Company party travelled along the Red Deer River to the height of land near the source of the river, close to present-day Skoki Valley. There they met the Kootenays – twenty-six men and four women, led by four elderly men. Together they headed to Rocky Mountain House, with Peigans constantly harassing the Kootenays. After reaching Rocky Mountain House, Thompson decided to send two of his men, Charles La Gasse and Pierre Le Blanc, back across the mountains with the Kootenays to spend the winter trapping and trading. With the chief's promise to return the following spring to show him the way across the mountains, Thompson even loaned him a horse, as all of the Kootenay horses had been stolen by the Peigans.

The route the Kootenays used to reach the height of land where they were met by David Thompson is not known. Vermilion Pass (present-day Highway 93 south) is a likely route. Other than Kicking Horse Pass (present-day Trans-Canada Highway), which was seldom used by the Natives, it is closest to the headwaters of the Red Deer River. Vermilion Pass also passes near the Paint Pots (in today's Kootenay National Park), which were well known to the Kootenays.

Once in the Bow Valley, the group would have chosen either Baker Creek or Corral Creek to take them to the headwaters of the Red Deer River. The Baker Creek trail was later used as an access point to Baker Lake and

Opposite: The Ya Ha Tinda Ranch grassland, surrounded by lofty peaks.

Below: The Red Deer River valley, looking west, with the trail high above the river.

beyond, especially by horse parties, but it had a reputation of being a "long, muddy, uninspiring trip."[15] The trail has since been decommissioned by Parks Canada for environmental reasons. While the Kootenays could have used this route, the Corral Creek trail, which archaeological digs indicate was used in prehistoric times, is a more likely choice. The trail would have followed close to the present-day route over Boulder Pass, past Baker Lake, and east of Fossil Mountain and Skoki Mountain to the Red Deer Lakes.

The trail along the Red Deer River from Ya Ha Tinda Ranch to the Bow Valley is of historic significance for three main reasons: one from the first period of exploration, one from the second, and one from the fourth. First, it is a traditional Aboriginal route across the mountains to the plains. This is why David Thompson brought the second period of exploration to the area: to meet the Kootenays on their way to Rocky Mountain House to trade. Finally, the route was used as an entry point to the mountains by explorer/mountaineer Professor A.P. Coleman some ninety-two years later.

Coleman's parties began at the Coleman ranch in Morley, entering the mountains along the Red Deer River. They then turned north along Divide Creek into the Clearwater drainage at today's Scotch Camp, where the old Cascade Fire Road turns east. Though they used this route several times in the late nineteenth and early twentieth centuries, there are no reports of other early tourists or explorers entering the mountains via the Red Deer River. Most outfitted trips to this region originated in the Bow Valley.

As for the old Native trail up Corral Creek and over Boulder Pass to the Ptarmigan Valley, Baker Lake, the Skoki Valley, and the headwaters of the Red Deer River – the route most likely followed by the Kootenay band that met David Thompson – there is no evidence of any non-Aboriginal use prior to the twentieth century. The 1885 completion of the Canadian Pacific Railway brought an influx of explorers, mountaineers, and tourists to Laggan (Lake Louise), but these explorers of the fourth period took their time in discovering this route.

The Red Deer River near Scotch Camp, where the old Cascade Fire Road turns south. This is a four-way junction in the trail, where travellers must choose whether to go north, south, or along the river.

The First Tourists

It was not until 1904 that Mary Schäffer,[16] a Philadelphia Quaker who had been coming to the Canadian Rockies since 1889, happened to hear of the Ptarmigan Valley. She and her late husband, Charles, had been collecting specimens in the vicinity of the railway for many years. Schäffer later wrote:

> I was under the impression that I knew every crack and cranny about Louise, every spot in which to find a rare plant, every place a woman could walk at least ten miles [16.1 kilometres] or ride fifty [eighty kilometres]. One day I heard by merest accident that Walter Dwight Wilcox of Washington, D.C., had rambled into a valley of which none of us had heard. To him it was probably only a pleasant walk and I think he returned at nightfall.[17]

Schäffer's mention of Wilcox's pleasant daytrip is the first reference to non-Native use of the Kootenay route. What Schäffer apparently did not know was that Wilcox and guide Bill Peyto[18] had travelled through the Skoki Valley and Baker Lake region as part of a trip from Mosquito Creek to Banff along the Sawback Range (see Route III on page 131). Wilcox was an astute observer and explorer, and his later trip into the Ptarmigan Valley was undoubtedly to look for a route from Lake Louise to the beautiful country he had seen in 1895 around Baker Lake and the Skoki Valley.

Schäffer's own adventures in the Ptarmigan Valley grew out of her and Charles's dream of completing a guide to the flora of the Canadian Rockies. Over the winter of 1903–1904 Schäffer resolved to complete the project, in hopes of mitigating the grief of having recently lost her mother, husband, and father. Realizing that her search for specimens would need to be broadened, Schäffer asked an old friend, outfitter Tom Wilson,[19] to recommend someone who could augment her minimal experience with horses and camping. Wilson recommended young Billy Warren, and in

Mary Schäffer, one of the first non-Aboriginal people to camp in the Ptarmigan Valley and the first woman to explore extensively in the Rocky Mountains.

September 1904, he took Schäffer; three friends, Misses Farr, Day, and James, all educators from Philadelphia; and a five-year-old girl on a week-long trip to the Ptarmigan Valley. The following year, they travelled over Boulder Pass and along the Red Deer River.[20] These are the first recorded overnight trips into the area.

Although it is unlikely that any traces of the old Native trail remained in 1904, the route was being revived by tourist explorers. As often happened, surveyors from the department of the interior were not far behind the first explorers, and in this case, Arthur Wheeler – a government surveyor soon to become founding president of the Alpine Club of Canada (ACC) – and his assistants surveyed the area in 1906.

Opposite: A.O. Wheeler surveyed extensively in the mountains but was best known as the founding president of the Alpine Club of Canada.

Below: Walter Wilcox (r) with his Yale University climbing friends (l–r) Yandell Henderson, L.F. Frissel, and H.G. Warrington.

MOUNTAINEERS

After the railway's arrival in the Bow Valley in 1885, mountaineers became one of the main groups using existing trails and employing outfitters and their crews to create new trails. Though the area between Laggan and the source of the Red Deer River was never popular during this period, a few mountaineers did leave their mark.

Late in August 1909, Canadian mountaineer J.W.A. Hickson crossed Boulder Pass into the Ptarmigan Valley. Compared to the band of Kootenays who likely used this route to meet David Thompson – or even Mary Schäffer's 1904 party – Hickson was travelling light. Intent on climbing Mount Douglas, he brought only two Swiss guides,[21] a packer, and several pack horses. In his own words:

> in a day's march (we) reached a camping ground in Baker Creek Valley about four hours' tramp from the base of the mountain. But alas! The weather, which looked none too favorable when we set out, grew steadily worse on the following days. Almost hourly snow flurries succeeded one another for the next thirty-six hours, which on the higher peaks deposited a foot of fresh snow, and rendered the vertical cliffs of Mt. Douglas, which were closely inspected, too dangerous to attempt, coated as they became when the weather cleared up with a treacherous verglas from the melting snow higher up. After several days ... we were obliged to return to Lake Louise.[22]

Undaunted, Hickson returned the following July, again accompanied by two Swiss guides, Edward Feuz Sr. and his son Edward. This time he expanded his party somewhat, bringing two packers, four horses, and food for ten days. As he explained in his journal, "We made good time to our camping ground which was reached in about six hours from Lake Louise, the trail being in quite excellent order. ... During the later part of the trip one passes Ptarmigan and Baker lakes, which are connected and lie in a large bed just beyond the top of Ptarmigan [Boulder] Pass."[23] When the mountaineers left for Mount Douglas, the packers were instructed to move camp to the head of the Red Deer River. This time the climb was successful and the whole party left the area by travelling down the Little Pipestone Creek and Pipestone River to Laggan.

J.W.A. Hickson (1873–1956)

Joseph William Andrew Hickson was born into a well-to-do Montreal family. He followed his early private school education with an arts degree from McGill in 1893, winning the gold medal in philosophy. He received his Ph.D. in philosophy, metaphysics and logic in Germany in 1900 and joined the faculty at McGill University the following year.[24]

Hickson was one of few Canadians to take an active interest in mountaineering in the early twentieth century. He and Swiss guide Edward Feuz Jr. climbed for five seasons in Europe and seventeen in the Rockies and Selkirks. Hickson was not physically robust, and a childhood accident had left him with a weak leg. Nevertheless, his iron will enabled him to climb until the age of fifty-seven. Over a period of twenty-five years, he and Feuz made many long expeditions in the Rockies, leading to more than thirty first ascents of major peaks. Feuz estimated they climbed between two and three hundred mountains together.

Hickson was an eccentric man with a brilliant and independent mind. While he and his mountain guide developed a strong friendship, he did not always agree with his colleagues – a fact that contributed to his rather early retirement in 1924. Throughout his life, Hickson was a prolific writer who contributed many articles on mountaineering and philosophy. He also took an active part in community life and presided over many clubs. He joined the Alpine Club of Canada in 1908, served as president from 1924–26

and as editor of the *Canadian Alpine Journal* for another two years. For many years, the annual meeting of the Montreal section of the ACC was held at his house, including the spring meeting of 1956, just a few months before his death. Hickson remained a bachelor all his life and died in 1956 at the age of eighty-three.

In 1911 the area at the head of the Red Deer River saw even more activity than during Hickson's 1909 and 1910 visits. Mountaineer James Foster Porter and eleven mountaineering friends thoroughly explored the region, naming many mountains, lakes, creeks, and valleys as they went.[25] Jimmy Simpson, a well-known outfitter, trapper, hunter, and explorer, served as

Opposite: Canadian mountaineer J.W.A. Hickson, the first to climb in the Ptarmigan Valley area, with his favourite Swiss guide, Edward Feuz Jr.

Below: Jimmy Simpson, one of the leading guides and outfitters in the Canadian Rockies.

guide and outfitter. At the end of July, the group journeyed past Ptarmigan Lake to the waterfall at the outlet of Baker Lake. There they set up camp and stayed for three weeks.

While exploring the valleys and meadows near the headwaters of the Red Deer River, Porter recounted:

> High up on our right a group of four tower-like rocks, each several hundred feet high, standing alone and as many more that had recently toppled over added greatly to the weird effect and reminded us of an old ruined castle (one that Merlin the Magician might have inhabited). It was suggested that Merlin Castle would be a good name for the mountain and Merlin Lake for the large lake.[26]

Near Merlin Lake, Porter and friends came across a marshy area with brachiopod fossils. Porter's land near Chicago was swampy and also housed such fossils, and he had named it Skokie, after the Potawatomi word for marshy. He felt that the name was equally suited to the area near Merlin Lake and the mountain above it. Somehow the spelling was later changed to Skoki, which also became the name of the creek and valley extending from the marsh.[27]

Perhaps as a result of Porter's vivid descriptions and Wheeler's earlier survey work, the Alpine Club of Canada held their 1915 camp in the Ptarmigan Valley. From July 13 to 26, the camp "was pitched in the little valley of Phacelia Lake (Hidden Lake), below Mt Richardson, running into that of Corral Creek, and was not visible until it was almost reached. The site of the camp was a beautiful one, affording magnificent views of the mountains of the Bow Valley. ... The next day the weather changed, and the Club 'enjoyed' the worst experience of the kind it ever suffered in camp. Heavy falls of wet snow rendered climbing too dangerous to be attempted and camp conditions by no means of the pleasantest."[28] Owing to war conditions the attendance was much smaller than usual, with a total of 103 ACC members walking or riding the trail from Lake Louise to a tent camp of sufficient size to hold the members and those attending to them.[29]

JAMES FOSTER PORTER (1871–1939)

James Foster Porter was a shy and private man, a person of great intellect and devotion to task. Originally from New England, he and his mother moved to Illinois when he was five years old. He obtained a masters degree in biology at Harvard but found no pleasure in his subsequent career in the field. He shifted gears, proceeding to study architecture at Columbia and later at Chicago. His main accomplishment as an architect was to build a Greek Revival home for his family in the town of Winnetka on the shores of Lake Michigan, just north of Chicago. He filled the home with plaster casts of classical sculpture and reproductions of great European paintings. Yet despite his academic credentials, he spent most of his life managing his mother's Chicago-based real-estate holdings, which he eventually inherited.

His first trip to the Canadian Rockies was in 1895, when he joined Walter Wilcox and Robert Barrett on their trip to Mount Assiniboine. He enjoyed the trip so much he began spending four to six weeks in the Rockies each summer. He married social activist Ruth Wadsworth Furness in 1898 and they had five children. Fourteen years into their marriage, he purchased a summer home on Great Spruce Head Island at Penobscot Bay, Maine. This purchase, unfortunately, curtailed his trips to the mountains. After 1912 he came only infrequently.

PARK WARDENS

Access to the Alpine Club of Canada camp was greatly facilitated by the trail the Warden Service had cut into the Ptarmigan Valley in 1914. Such trails were intended to facilitate park patrol, as were the cabins the wardens built alongside them. In 1916 Commissioner of National Parks James Harkin ordered the wardens to identify their cabins with signs and to erect trail signs indicating location and distances to warden cabins. Fearing that easily followed trails might reduce tourists' dependence on their business, guides and outfitters protested this development. Several of the signs near Banff were destroyed, and the wardens posted no new ones. Nevertheless, wardens continued to leave the cabins unlocked for travellers' use until 1929 and outhouses were accessible to backcountry users until quite recently, when locks began appearing.

In 1921 explorer/mountaineer Walter Wilcox, the first non-Native reported to have travelled into the Ptarmigan Valley, made use of one of the earliest warden cabins.[30] He and A.L. Castle followed Corral Creek to the Red Deer Warden Cabin, built prior to 1912. The next morning they forded the Red Deer River, with packer Fred Stephens guiding the pack train. The party pushed through heavy timber until they reached Douglas Lake. They observed what appeared to be twenty-year-old blaze marks on the trees, but could find no sign of human presence beyond the lake. Wilcox was the first non-Aboriginal person to explore the area south of Douglas Lake, which he named the Valley of Hidden Lakes.

Opposite: Mountaineer J.F. Porter extensively explored the Ptarmigan and Skoki valley areas.

Right: James Harkin, first Commissioner of the National Parks Branch, was instrumental in the establishment of the Warden Service and a strong advocate for conservation.

Douglas Lake, first visited by Walter Wilcox in 1921, remains virtually untouched by humans.

SCIENTISTS

Very little of the third period of exploration – that of the scientists and surveyors – took place along this route. Much of the early survey work in the mountains was associated with the Canadian Pacific Railway. Because the Bow and North Saskatchewan rivers were the most obvious entry points, railway engineers did not consider the Red Deer River as a possible route into the mountains. Nevertheless, the federal government did ask a few scientists to survey and detail the natural features of the area. Dr. George Mercer Dawson,[31] future director of the Geological Survey of Canada, was assigned to conduct a geological survey of the eastern Rockies. In 1884, he followed David Thompson's route from Scotch Camp, located on the Red Deer River at the junction of Snow Creek (see Route IV on page 168), westward to the headwaters of the Red Deer River then on to the Bow Valley.

In keeping with his profession, Dawson often gave detailed accounts of the geology, meteorology, ethnology, and flora of the country he travelled. Unfortunately, his attention to detail did not extend to his description of the routes he followed. Thus, little is known of his trip up the Cascade River and west along the Red Deer to the Bow River. It is unlikely that Dawson took the old Native route through the Ptarmigan Valley and down Corral Creek. More likely he continued west from the Red Deer Lakes along Little Pipestone Creek and the Pipestone River to the Bow River.

Nearly twenty years later, in 1917, the federal government instructed Dominion Land Surveyor Morrison P. Bridgland and his inexperienced assistant, D.L.S. Ley Harris, to spend the next four years surveying in the area north and south of the Red Deer River. Bridgland, an experienced ACC climbing guide, patiently taught his understudy how to climb. After the first ascent, Harris recalled vividly the panoramic view of the clouds over the Red Deer River. On another climb, the pair surveyed Wilcox's Valley of the Hidden Lakes from peaks at the head of the Panther Valley. Later that summer the two surveyors made a very difficult climb on a mountain north of the Red Deer River. Bridgland honoured his young assistant by naming the mountain after him.

Dr. George Mercer Dawson of the Geological Survey of Canada had completed a geological survey of the eastern Rockies by 1884.

MORRISON P. BRIDGLAND (1878–1948)

Born on a farm on the outskirts of Toronto, Morrison Bridgland received his early education at the Toronto Junction Collegiate Institute. After graduation, he went to Victoria College at the University of Toronto, where he played football and graduated with honours in mathematics and physics in 1901.

His powerful athletic build was to serve him well. Following a year at the Ontario School of Practical Sciences at the University of Toronto, Bridgland went west to assist A.O. Wheeler with his surveying work. Bridgland worked in the mountains from 1902 to 1931, gaining a reputation as a tireless and thorough worker in the pitching of camp, packing of horses, cutting of wood – all the "chores" of survey work. E.O. Wheeler stated: "I have met few men who so consistently subordinated their own inclinations to the achievement of the object."[32] The output resulting from the survey work was detailed and accurate maps of extensive areas of the Rockies, and his treatise on photographic surveying became an authoritative work on the subject.

Bridgland's climbing skill, combined with his study of mountains and thoroughly sound judgment also made him an exceptional mountaineer, equalled by few. A founding member of the Alpine Club of Canada, he attended its first camp and later served as a guide, leading many climbs. He made several hundred ascents over the course of his lifetime, preferring the Brazeau region above all others. Bridgland's obituary in the *Canadian Alpine Journal* declared that he had "climbed more peaks and pioneered more trails than any other Canadian."[33]

M.P. Bridgland, third from the left, with fellow guides (l–r): Edward Feuz, H.G. Wheeler, and Gottfried Feuz at the 1906 ACC camp in the Yoho Valley.

Whereas Dr. Dawson spent little time recording where he actually travelled, Dr. Charles Doolittle Walcott[34] left extensive records of the geological expeditions that led him throughout the Rocky Mountains. This world-renowned geologist and palaeontologist, secretary to the Smithsonian Institution, first visited the Canadian Rockies with his wife, Helena, and their two youngest children, Helen and Stuart, in the summer of 1907. For the next eighteen years Walcott spent every summer collecting fossils and studying the geology of the Rockies. He used the old Aboriginal trail to the Ptarmigan Valley as an entry point for many of these trips.

The Walcotts conducted their travels somewhat differently than most travellers of their time. They did not follow the custom of hiring an outfitter to provide horses, camp equipment, food, supplies, a cook, and men to manage the horses and perform camp chores. Instead they kept their own string of horses, which were sometimes wintered with the park wardens' horses at Ya Ha Tinda Ranch and sometimes in Shelby, Montana.

However, that is not to say that the Walcotts did much of the camp work. Their full-time faithful servant Arthur Brown managed the trips very efficiently and was reputed to be an excellent cook. Each year, Walcott hired one or two packers to assist in setting up and dismantling camps, handling the horses, and performing other chores. Walcott's well-organized outfit made its first foray along part of the old Kootenay/Thompson trail when he and his son, Stuart, followed in Mary Schäffer's footsteps from Laggan and the Ptarmigan Valley in 1909. Walcott repeated the trip in 1916 with his third wife, Mary Vaux Walcott;[35] camp manager Arthur Brown; and packer Alex Mitton. With his 1916 group of travellers, Walcott returned to a beautiful spot at the foot of Ptarmigan Peak to set up camp. Walcott declared: "Am glad to camp here with Mary as it is a beautiful spot & Stuart & I camped here about 1909."[36]

The ride to the camp had been difficult, and the group took advantage of a rainy morning to stay in camp and rest the following day. Walcott continued some geological studies begun on his 1909 trip, while Mary undoubtedly searched for new wildflowers to identify, paint, and photograph. On August 10, they ascended Ptarmigan Pass (Boulder Pass) and spent the day fruitlessly searching for fossils. After a short stay, they moved on to the area west of Lake Louise.[37]

But the Ptarmigan Valley had not seen the last of the Walcotts. Returning to the region each summer from 1921 to 1925, the Walcotts left their mark both literally and figuratively. In 1921 the Walcotts' packers and trail cutters, Billy Lewis and Cecil Smith, cut a trail up Baker Creek to the Wildflower Creek valley, just south of Baker Lake. Their efforts proved enormously profitable to Mary Vaux Walcott's wildflower studies: during

Dr. Charles Doolittle Walcott spent eighteen years studying geology and collecting fossils in the Canadian Rockies.

their two days in the valley, she identified eighty-two types of flowers within two hundred feet (sixty-one metres) of the tent![38] They proceeded to the Red Deer Lakes then northwest to the Castleguard Meadows.[39]

On August 8, 1922, the Walcotts returned to their previous year's camp on the Red Deer River – near the spot where, 122 years earlier, David Thompson had met the Kootenay band. This time the Walcotts arrived from the north, having travelled through the Clearwater Valley and over Pipestone Pass (see Route II on page 73). Again, Mary painted wildflowers while Charles studied the geology of nearby formations and proofread scientific papers. Paul Stevens and William Shea joined them as helpers and packers.

That year, the Walcotts left a legacy in the valley by having Paul Stevens cut a trail to Douglas Lake. On August 20 the party followed the rough, slow trail – which no doubt followed the trail made by the Wilcox party the previous year – to the upper end of Douglas Lake. On August 29 they returned to the Red Deer River camp, and in early September they were back in Lake Louise.

That fall, back in Washington, Walcott wrote: "This beautiful valley [Douglas Lake valley] is only 12 to 15 miles [nineteen to twenty-four kilometres] in a direct line east and north-east of Lake Louise Station. ... This superb canyon valley with its forests, lakes, glaciers, and mountain walls and peaks should be opened up to the mountain tourist who has the energy to ride along a fine Rocky Mountain trail from Lake Louise."[40] However, the area was never opened up to tourists as Walcott suggested and is as wild and remote today as it was in the early twentieth century.

The Walcotts followed their 1922 explorations of the unspoiled Douglas Lake area with a season in the more settled Columbia Valley near Radium Hot Springs. But they could not resist returning to the Baker Lake area. They travelled to Lake Louise at the end of the season, then followed the now well-established trail over Boulder Pass and through the Ptarmigan Valley. They spent September 10–18 collecting fossils and photographing geological formations around Baker Lake.[41]

The Walcotts continued these studies the following summer; on July 25, 1924, they followed the Ptarmigan Valley trail to the previous year's campsite on Baker Creek. The ever-reliable camp manager and cook Arthur Brown accompanied them from Washington, and Tex Wood and Dan Derrick joined them as packers.[42] Again, Charles collected fossils on Brachiopod and Fossil mountains while Mary painted wildflowers. On August 19, Charles's journal notes, "We packed up and moved to our 'Wild Flower' camp of 1921. A warm day in the sunshine, The trail was not bad. By 4:00 P.M. our tent was in order & Arthur had a good dinner at 6:30."[43] This was one of their better days.

The summer had been plagued by bad weather. Walcott complained that the poor conditions prevented him from working: "Am not able to climb so I have to make old Cricket [his horse] take [me] up as high as the going will permit."[44] After more than a week of rain, they moved camp back to Baker Lake, but the rain and mist persisted. At the end of August they followed the Red Deer River to today's Scotch Camp, where the old Cascade Fire Road turns east (see Route IV on page 180). A few days later, they continued along the old David Thompson trail to Eagle Creek, east of Ya Ha Tinda Ranch, which Walcott simply called "the government ranch." The Walcotts spent the night at the ranch house, then continued to the campsite on the Red Deer River for their respective studies. By mid-September the end of another season had them following the Red Deer River trail back to Lake Louise.

Once the snows were safely melted, the Walcotts returned to Lake Louise for another season of study. On July 8, 1925, they returned to their 1916 camp at Ptarmigan (Boulder) Pass, following the well-worn Aboriginal trail the Warden Service had upgraded in 1914. This time, they had fifteen horses, with Tex Wood, Bill Lewis, and Arthur Brown assisting. The couple spent the remainder of the summer photographing, collecting, painting, and studying. They moved camp several times to well-known spots near the Skoki Valley, the Red Deer River, Baker Lake, and Wildflower Pond.[45] On September 14, the Walcott party returned to Lake Louise. A week later they returned home from what was to be Charles Walcott's last trip to the Canadian Rockies. He died in 1927 at the age of seventy-six.

Escorted Outfitted Trips

While the Walcotts were conducting their scientific studies, the Red Deer River region was also being explored by a new breed of tourist: participants in the increasingly popular escorted backcountry trips. These trips differed from the usual outfitted trips in that the route was planned by the escort.[46] Participants, who were recruited by advertising, often did not even know one another prior to the trip.

Caroline Hinman's Off the Beaten Track trips are a fine example of these excursions. Hinman herself had been bitten by the travel bug as a teenager. She began her career leading trips in Europe, but after participating in Curly Phillips's excursions north of Mount Robson she could not resist the call of the Rockies. In 1916 she led her first North American trip, to Glacier National Park in Montana. She then turned her attention northward. For the next forty years she offered a wilderness experience in the Canadian Rockies to groups of ten to twelve wealthy American girls, often conducting three outings each summer.[47]

Hinman first escorted an excursion to the Canadian Rockies in 1917. The party included Ulysses LaCasse as guide; Jim Boyce, Max Brooks, and Howard Deegan as assistants; and nine teenaged girls. The three-week circle trip concluded by following Snow Creek (the old Cascade Fire Road, see Route IV on page 180) north to Scotch Camp, then travelling west along the Red Deer River on the old David Thompson trail. Following Hinman's strategy of travelling for a few days and then spending a day or two relaxing in an interesting spot, the group followed the Red Deer River August 23 and 24, rested in the Ptarmigan Valley for three days, then returned to Lake Louise on August 28.[48]

A decade passed before another Off the Beaten Track tour followed the Red Deer River. Hinman's 1927 guests included mountaineer Lillian Gest and her friend Margaret Hill. Gest and Hinman had met in 1923 and made at least one trip together every year between 1924 and 1934. Jim Boyce, a Banffite who guided for Caroline for sixteen summers, was head guide. With him were Charlie Hunter as head packer, Bert Mickel as cook, four assistants, and Jim's wife, Ada. There were also eleven other paying customers, for a total of twenty-two in the group.

Caroline Hinman, leader of Off the Beaten
Track alpine adventures for American girls.

The party arrived in Lake Louise on July 1, then followed Mary Schäffer's footsteps along the now popular tourist trail up Corral Creek to the Ptarmigan Valley. Nevertheless, as Lillian Gest later wrote, the area was still a far cry from today's backcountry destination: "There was no Temple Lodge, no half-way hut, no Skoki Lodge and few people knew of the area."[49]

The group spent three nights camped in the Ptarmigan Valley before passing through some of the Walcotts' favourite Baker Lake haunts en route to the Red Deer River. They followed the valley to present-day Scotch Camp, at the approach to the Divide Summit trail (see Route IV on page 168). After a one-day layover, they proceeded north toward the Clearwater Valley. Caroline Hinman returned to the Ptarmigan Valley/Red Deer River trails three times in the 1930s.[50]

Below: Jim Boyce dedicated sixteen summers to guiding Caroline Hinman's Off the Beaten Track tours.

Opposite: Baker Lake, from the ridge between Baker and Ptarmigan lakes. Today's campground is located at the far end of Baker Lake.

Artists

After mountaineers and hunters began following the trails to their respective destinations and tourist/explorers began enjoying the mountain wonders by horseback, it was only a matter of time before artists discovered the Ptarmigan Valley. Artists had been painting mountain scenes ever since the rail lines were built – often at the request of railway officials who used their paintings both to decorate rail cars and hotels and in advertising campaigns to draw more visitors to the mountains.[51]

The first artist to venture into the Ptarmigan Valley was Carl Rungius. In August 1910, when the valley was known only to a few explorers such as Walter Wilcox and Mary Schäffer, the famous wildlife artist was drawn by an invitation from art-loving outfitter and guide Jimmy Simpson.[52] After seeing a Rungius painting of Dall sheep reproduced in an outdoor magazine, Simpson wrote inviting him to come and paint Rocky Mountain Bighorn sheep. Rungius accepted, and the two followed in Mary Schäffer's footsteps along the old Native trail over Boulder Pass into the Ptarmigan Valley. Their week in the valley initiated Rungius's long association with the Rocky Mountains. He returned to the valley for four days in July 1912. In the 1930s, Rungius returned often to the Ptarmigan Valley to paint.[53]

The Ptarmigan Valley was also a favourite location for landscape painter and portraitist Lars Haukaness. Haukaness moved to Calgary in

1926 (from Norway via Chicago and Winnipeg) and immediately began painting in the Canadian Rockies. He was described by friend Archie Key in July 1929 as "an elderly man with a yellowish-white beard and dressed in an old grey coat, khaki riding breeches and puttees. Behind his spectacles, which perched insecurely on his nose, there was a humorous twinkle in his eyes. He was full of enthusiasm, preparing to leave for a sketching trip [to the Ptarmigan Valley] in the Canadian Rockies."[54]

On that trip, Haukaness suffered a heart attack at his favourite sketching spot on Ptarmigan Lake. He died on the old Boulder Pass trail while returning to Lake Louise. His obituary read in part: "While riding to Lake Louise, after having been stricken mortally ill with heart disease in his lonely teepee in Ptarmigan Valley, Lars Haukaness, 66 years of age, ... fell dead from his horse about three miles [4.8 kilometres] from the resort, early Wednesday morning. His dog, 'Bragg,' returning to the town without his master, gave the police a clue to the tragedy."[55]

Other artists who travelled through the Ptarmigan Valley to the Skoki area prior to 1930 were Belmore Brown, a New Yorker who bought property in Banff in the 1920s, and Lawren Harris, a member of the Group of Seven who painted in the mountains between 1924 and 1929 and stayed in the Skoki Valley on at least one of these trips.

The region east of today's village of Lake Louise, encompassing the Ptarmigan Valley, Skoki Valley, and the Baker Lake and Red Deer Lakes region, remains a popular tourist destination. The combined attractions of many small lakes and mountain passes with extensive alpine meadows and abundant wildlife have led to heavy use of the region's trails. The trail over Boulder Pass, probably used by the Kootenays in 1800 when they were met by David Thompson near the headwaters of the Red Deer River, is still the main route into the area. Each year – summer and winter – hundreds of visitors follow on this well-worn trail, identified by Walter Wilcox and popularized by Mary Schäffer.

Carl Rungius, artist, hunter, and mountain explorer.

The Trail Today

The journey from Ya Ha Tinda Ranch to the village of Lake Louise is a very pleasant hike of three to six or more days and is suitable for hikers of any age. There are no high passes – and therefore no spectacular mountain vistas – but this trail provides some of the best river valley hiking the Rockies have to offer. Several creek crossings are not bridged, but they are usually only calf-deep and will not present problems to careful hikers. Normal caution should be exercised during spring runoff and after periods of heavy rain.

The most difficult part of this hike may be arranging transportation. If one chooses to start or finish at the east end, someone has to drive the gravel Forestry Trunk Road and Ya Ha Tinda access road from the old Highway 1A to the ranch. These roads are generally in good condition and present no real driving challenges. My wife, Cheryl, did not relish the thought of driving the narrow, winding gravel road alone after dropping me off at the ranch, but she found the solitary drive back over rarely used roads easier than expected. Portions of the trail can also be hiked by entering or exiting the trail along the Sawback Range (see Route III on page 129) or using the Cascade Fire Road/Divide Creek trail (see Route IV on page 167).

The hike begins on the rolling grasslands of Ya Ha Tinda Ranch. The gap between Wapiti Mountain and Warden Rock through which the Red Deer River exits the mountains is visible in the distance. After entering the mountains, the valley initially narrows then widens beyond Scotch Camp. Much of the trail is on a bench high above the river and provides excellent views of the surrounding mountains. At times it does descend to river level; some sections pass through heavily wooded areas.

The historic trail to scenic Douglas Lake is a worthwhile side trip. Hiking this trail involves fording the Red Deer River, but the river is braided near the crossing and should not present any difficulty except during spring runoff and periods of heavy rain. Normal caution is required during periods of high water flow.

The modern trail along the Red Deer River to this point is probably geographically close to the route followed by David Thompson and his party, as the nature of the terrain would have made passage relatively easy even prior to trail clearing. The Thompson party's trip south through the foothills to the Red Deer River and west along the Red Deer to the height of land where he met the band of Kootenays has been traced in detail by Joyce and Peter McCart in *On the Road with David Thompson*.[56]

At the headwaters of the Red Deer River, the trail turns south through the narrow valley of Cotton Grass Pass then west again through a narrow gap to beautiful Baker and Ptarmigan lakes. It then drops over Boulder Pass to the Halfway Hut and on to Lake Louise. Most hikers will want to spend some time in the area south and west of the Red Deer Lakes, staying in the campsites provided and exploring the many lakes and valleys in the surrounding area.

An added advantage for hikers in the Skoki Valley is that they can experience traditional route-finding methods first-hand. In the early days of exploration in the Rocky Mountains, men often climbed mountains in order to determine the lay of the land and to get a good bearing on where they could find passage through what often appeared, from valley level, to be a maze of mountains. The panorama you can witness from the top of Skoki Mountain is an excellent example of the fabulous views available from the summit of even a modest mountain, especially because it is an isolated peak and offers a 360° view.

I recently had the opportunity to climb Skoki Mountain while spending a few delightful days at Skoki Lodge with Cheryl. The climb is demanding but not particularly difficult, and from the top, the height of land mentioned by David Thompson in 1800 is clearly visible. The Red Deer Lakes can be seen to the northeast and the stream that flows from them forms part of the headwaters of the Red Deer River, which continues east, eventually flowing into Hudson Bay and the North Atlantic Ocean via the Saskatchewan River.

From Skoki's summit you will also be able to see the drainage of Little Pipestone Creek to the northwest (see Route III on page 139). These waters flow into the Bow River and eventually join the waters from the Red Deer River as part of the Saskatchewan River. And, to the south, the route leading to Deception Pass (Route III below) is clearly visible, as well as the Merlin Lake/Merlin Meadows area to the southwest. This southerly view is somewhat unique in that both Merlin Lake and the Skoki Lakes (near Deception Pass) can be seen at the same time, although they are separated by a substantial mountain, the Wall of Jericho. To the southeast, Cotton Grass Pass is clearly visible, leading to the Baker Lake drainage and the route to Boulder Pass.

The area between the ranch and the Red Deer Lakes is designated as a random camping area in which you can camp in any suitable spot that is at least five kilometres from the nearest trailhead, fifty metres off the trail, and seventy metres from the nearest water source. There are endless suitable camping spots all along the Red Deer River. Old outfitters' camps are often ideal, with good sources of water and plenty of relatively flat spots to put up a tent. Many have bear poles for food storage, and some even offer a makeshift privy. These camps are also pleasing to the senses, many having been established in scenic locations. We have indicated the location of the obvious ones in the trail guide below. From the Red Deer Lakes to the end of the hike, Parks Canada provides campsites at the Red Deer Lakes, Baker Lake, and the Halfway Hut.

The Red Deer Lakes, source of the Red Deer River, and the Red Deer River valley from Skoki Mountain.

Trail Guide

Distances are adapted from existing trail guides: Patton and Robinson, Potter, and Beers, and from Gem-Trek maps. Distances intermediate from those given in the sources are estimated from topographical maps and from hiking times. All distances are in kilometres.

Ya Ha Tinda Road to Fish Creek Parking Lot
(Lake Louise)

Maps   82 O/12 Barrier Mountain
82 N/9 Hector Lake
82 N/8 Lake Louise (Lake Louise and Yoho, Gem Trek)

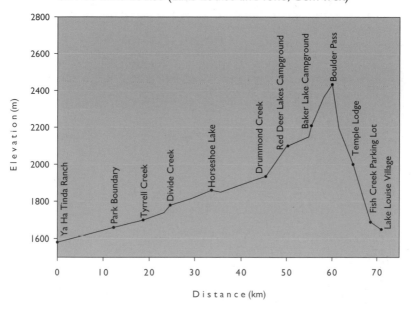

Trailhead

From Highway 940, the Forestry Trunk Road, turn west onto the Ya Ha Tinda road immediately north of the Red Deer River bridge and follow the gravel road west 23 km to the ranch. The parking area is opposite the Bighorn Creek Campground and is 1.5 km before the trailhead. From the west, exit the Trans-Canada Highway at the Lake Louise interchange and proceed uphill on the Whitehorn Road, past highway 1A on the right. Turn right on the Fish Creek gravel road and follow the road to the parking lot, less than 3 km from the Trans-Canada Highway.

0.0   Ya Ha Tinda road junction.

0.2   Scalp Creek. After the ankle-deep ford, continue west along the old Cascade Fire Road through the open prairie of Ya Ha Tinda Ranch.

5.0   The trail follows along a high bench overlooking the Red Deer River with beautiful views.

5.9   Ranch fence with a gate. Continue travelling through flat mountain prairie country.

10.0   Sign for the west boundary of the ranch, which reads "Ya Ha Tinda Horse Ranch." The trail has now passed through the gap into the mountains but is still fairly open with great views all round.

11.3   Wagon road on the left leads into Melcher's Ranch. Excellent coffee!

12.3   Park Boundary. Once inside the park, the old fire road looks more like a trail. Continue along an old burn area beside the river in a fairly narrow valley with great views.

18.7   Tyrrell Creek. An easy ford.

23.2   Junction. The Red Deer River trail continues ahead; the Cascade Fire Road turns south and crosses a substantial river bridge. Scotch Camp is at the junction of the road and bridge, just after you cross the bridge. On the Red Deer River trail, an old wooden sign points west and reads "Clearwater River, Horseshoe Lake, and Lake Louise via Temple." Follow the sign, continuing west on the trail, which initially follows a high bench above the river.

24.6	Divide Creek. After an easy ford, you arrive at an old outfitter's camp just west of the creek.

24.6   Divide Creek. After an easy ford, you arrive at an old outfitter's camp just west of the creek.

24.8   Divide/Peters Creek trail branches to the right. An old white painted sign points north to the "Clearwater River, 22 miles [35.4 km]." Continue straight ahead. There are good views from the bench above the river.

29.3   Easy ford of McConnell Creek.

33.6   Horseshoe (Skeleton) Lake trail is on the left. An old painted sign reads "Horseshoe Lake, 1 mi. [1.6 km]" Continue ahead.

35.5   Red Deer gorge and waterfall.

37.3   Easy ford of Tributary Creek.

37.7   Red Deer Warden Cabin. There is a wooden fence and gate just before and after the cabin.

41.9   Old campsite with firewood cut up, ready to go, when I was there. The trail continues through heavy forest some distance from the river.

43.5   Just beyond a small lake by the river, an old sign reads "Douglas Lake," which is on the south side of the Red Deer River. There are two old outfitter camps at the junction. The trail to Lake Louise continues ahead. You now have two options:

To take a side trip to Douglas Lake, cross the river at a braided area near the first sign then follow the riverbank to the opposite side of the meadow where there is another sign in the trees that also reads "Douglas Lake." The well-marked trail heads into the woods and twists and turns its way along what looks like a natural path, likely the one made by Walter Wilcox in 1921. The trail reaches the lakeshore approximately one-third of the way along the lake from the north end.

If you move along to Lake Louise, bear in mind that after the sign to Douglas Lake, continuing south and west, the trail is practically non-existent. Just follow the river across a big open area and pick up a good trail again at the end. There is another waterfall in the river here.

45.0 Unused wooden fence and gate across the trail. The terrain opens up into a large meadow.

45.4 Drummond Creek ford. At first glance, the creek, which flows in from the north, appears to be the Red Deer River. Since there is an old horse trail continuing along beside the creek, you may be inclined to follow it. This leads only to a dead-end valley. The Red Deer River turns to the left (south) at this point, and the Red Deer River trail follows the river. It is important to ford Drummond Creek at this junction, then follow the river south.

48.1 Natural Bridge trail branches to the left. This side trail leads through a wooded area and reaches the Natural Bridge in 2.5 km.

49.4 New fence, gate across the trail. Before the fence is a sign that points to a horse camp.

49.9 Cyclone Warden Cabin. A short distance beyond the cabin is a trail junction. Turn left (south) toward the Red Deer Lakes Campground and Baker Lake. There is another sign pointing to the horse camp.

50.3 Red Deer Lakes Campground (Sk19).

50.8 Trail to Skoki Valley via Jones Pass goes to the right (west). The trail to Baker Lake continues ahead and passes through a gap between two mountains before traversing Cotton Grass Pass.

52.1 Trail to Skoki Valley (shortcut) via Jones Pass goes to the right (west). Continue ahead through very open country with virtually no trees. The trail heads toward a gap where it turns right (west) again toward Baker Lake.

54.8 Turn right (west) for Baker Lake. The trail ahead goes to the Pulsatilla Valley.

55.4   Baker Lake Campground (Sk11). From the campground the trail follows an open valley along the north shore of Baker Lake. It is wet near the west end of the lake. Continue toward Ptarmigan Lake.

58.1   Trail junction. The trail to the right (north) leads to the Skoki Valley and Deception Pass. Keep left (south) for Lake Louise.

60.0   Top of Boulder Pass. The Lake Louise ski trails can be seen from here, on the right (west side of the valley).

61.5   Trail junction. The trail to Hidden Lake, Hidden Lake Campground (Sk5), and Halfway Hut is on the right (west).

62.3   Corral Creek meadows. The trail along here is wide and heavily used.

64.7   Temple Lodge. There is a signpost at the trailhead uphill from Temple Lodge. Continue ahead across the ski run and follow the Temple access road to the Fish Creek parking lot.

68.6   Fish Creek parking lot. Turn left along the Ski Louise access road to the village of Lake Louise, approximately 2 km.

The hiker trail from Baker Lake campground skirts the shore of Ptarmigan Lake.

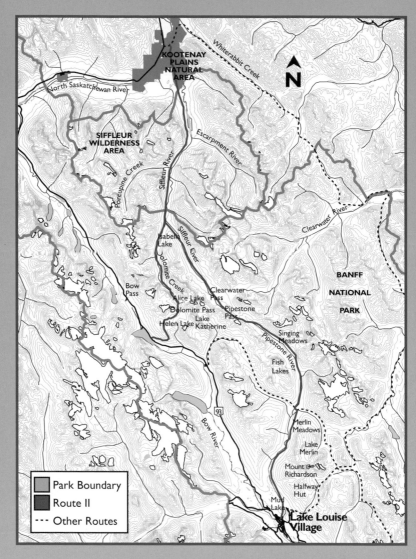

Route II from Lake Louise to the North Saskatchewan River over Pipestone Pass and along the Siffleur River

ROUTE II

A Northern Passage: Dr. James Hector's Route
from Laggan (Lake Louise) to the Kootenay Plains

After hiking over Pipestone Pass and along the Siffleur River, I arrived at the Kootenay Plains parking area to find tourists milling around in a buzz of activity. As my wife, Cheryl, had not yet arrived to pick me up, I found a cool spot in the shade of a large tree. I have found that tourists often pay no attention to other people, even backpackers with grey beards. This time was an exception. One gentleman, probably in his fifties, approached me. His genuinely friendly demeanour made me think he was a small-town or country dweller. My hunch was proved correct as he soon revealed that his home was in rural Ontario, near Algonquin Park. He and his wife had been travelling across Canada in a small camper trailer. Amazed to discover that I had backpacked from Lake Louise, he offered food or anything else I might want. I was delighted to have him refill my water bottle with ice water! After four days of solitary hiking, his interesting conversation – and the ice water – made my day.

CHRONOLOGY

1859   Dr. James Hector becomes the first European man on record to travel from the Bow River to the North Saskatchewan River. He and his party traverse Pipestone Pass and follow the Siffleur River northward.

1859   Ten days after Hector passes through the area, James Carnegie, Earl of Southesk, completes his journey through the Front Ranges by crossing Pipestone Pass from the north and proceeding down the Bow River.

1892   R.G. McConnell uses Pipestone Pass as a route into the eastern foothills to search for coal. He surveys and makes a geological inventory from the foothills to Howse Pass.

1898   Rev. Harry Nicholls, Rev. Charles Noyes, Charles S. Thompson, and George M. Weed become the first mountaineers to proceed north along the Pipestone River. They and Ralph Edwards discover the route over Dolomite Pass to Bow Lake.

At about the same time, Bill Peyto guides mountaineers Norman Collie, Hugh Stutfield, and Herman Woolley over the Pipestone Pass route on a quest to reach Athabasca Pass.

1902   For the next six years, Tom Wilson herds horses to and from his ranch on the Kootenay Plains over Pipestone Pass.

1906   Mary Schäffer takes what is to become one of many extensive trips in the Rocky Mountains, this one over Pipestone Pass to visit the Stoneys on the Kootenay Plains.

1907   Martin Nordegg and Dr. D.B. Dowling use the Pipestone Pass route to the Kootenay Plains to enter the eastern foothills in search of coal.

1907   Arthur Coleman, Lucius Coleman, Rev. George Kinney, and Jack Boker use the Pipestone Pass route to the Kootenay Plains on their way to attempt Mount Robson.

1908   Nordegg establishes his headquarters in the Banff Springs Hotel and uses the Pipestone Pass route to access the Bighorn area of the foothills.

1908   Tom Wilson nearly loses his life crossing Pipestone Pass in a winter snowstorm.

1912   Martin Nordegg takes his daughter, Marcelle, to see the town of Nordegg and let her experience the trials of pack-train travel over Pipestone Pass.

1914   Nordegg crosses Pipestone Pass for the last time.

1920   Dr. Charles Walcott and Mary Vaux Walcott use the Pipestone Pass route to carry their studies to the Siffleur River.

       Val Fynn uses this route on a hunting trip to the Clearwater Valley in the fall. He returns to Lake Louise only five days after the Walcotts.

1925   Caroline Hinman uses the Pipestone Pass route near the beginning of an ambitious fifty-five-day expedition to Mount Robson. She repeats the trip over the pass in the fall on a hunting outing.

1926   Caroline Hinman, Lillian Gest, Louise Vincent, and Hal Learned use the Pipestone Pass route on a hunting trip to the Dolomite Valley, the Siffleur Valley, and the Kootenay Plains. They return to the area in each of the following two years.

History

Early Explorers

It was late in the summer of 1859. Captain John Palliser was in the Cypress Hills (in present-day southeastern Alberta), having just divided the members of his famous expedition into three groups. Two years earlier, the group of scientists and explorers consisting of Palliser, the leader of the expedition and an explorer; geologist, naturalist, and physician Dr. James Hector; botanical collector Eugene Bourgeau; astronomical observer John Sullivan, who acted as secretary of the group; and magnetical observer Lieutenant Thomas Blakiston, had set out on a trip across Canada together with a large number of assistants. They were to explore the region between Lake Superior and the Rocky Mountains. Within the mountains they focused on the passes south of the fur traders' Athabasca Pass and north of the 49th parallel.

Palliser charged Dr. Hector with exploring the Rocky Mountains north of the Bow River. He had spent the summer of 1858 exploring the Vermilion and Kicking Horse passes, surviving a variety of situations, including what at first seemed to be a fatal kick from a horse, hence the name of the latter pass. Now Hector was heading north again to the Bow Valley.

Hector's party consisted of James Beads, a Métis voyageur who was a personal servant of Sir George Simpson; three other men: McLaurin, Burnham, and Oliver Vanesse; Nimrod, a Stoney hunter and guide who had also accompanied Hector on his first trip; and Nimrod's wife. They had eighteen horses, nine of which were loaded with food for the journey: 250 pounds (113 kilograms) each of pemmican. Near the mouth of the Highwood River they met up with a Stoney band. Hector engaged one of them, a man known only as William, who also brought his wife along.[1] The party heading toward Old Bow Fort (on the Bow River along the west end of today's Stoney Reserve) now consisted of nine men and women.

They reached the fort in mid-August and proceeded up the Bow River. From the striking mass of rock that forms Cascade Mountain, Hector's party continued up the valley to the Vermilion Pass crossing, near the base of Castle Mountain. The previous year Hector had turned southward at that point to cross Vermilion Pass. This year he wanted to remain on the east side of the Rockies as long as possible. He was hoping to find a more northerly route across the Continental Divide, perhaps near the headwaters of the North Saskatchewan River.

Hector halted near Castle Mountain to hold council with his Native guides. William proposed following an established Native route up the Pipestone River, over Pipestone Pass, and down the Siffleur River to the Kootenay Plains. There, he suggested, they would find ample sheep for food and perhaps a better trail. Hector concurred.

The party worked their way up the Pipestone River, passing a spectacular tooth-shaped mountain they could not resist naming Molar Mountain. Near the base of the pass, the Stoneys found some of the soft, fine-grained, grey-blue stone they used for making pipes. They called the creek *pa-hooh-to-hiagoo-pi-wap-ta* or Blue Pipestone River.[2]

The route over Pipestone Pass was very steep and rocky for the horses, but the far side offered a gentler path into a meadow-like valley. Hector named this new river Siffleur – the French name for the whistling marmots that were prevalent in the area. Following the river through thick and sometimes tangled woods to the broad valley of the North Saskatchewan River and out onto the Kootenay Plains, Hector became the first recorded European man to travel from the Bow River to the North Saskatchewan via Pipestone Pass.

Molar Mountain from the Pipestone Pass trail. The landmark's obvious resemblance to a tooth inspired its name.

The Siffleur Valley, looking north from the top of Pipestone Pass, with part of the hiking trail on the left. These rocky outcrops are home to the siffleurs, or whistling marmots.

SIR JAMES HECTOR (1834–1907)

James Hector was born in Edinburgh, Scotland, on March 16, 1834. After completing his initial schooling at age fourteen, he went to work in his father's law office. At eighteen, he enrolled in the medical school at Edinburgh University. In addition to medicine, he took courses in botany, chemistry, natural history, mineralogy, geology, and palaeontology; it was actually the option of taking these elective courses that had drawn him to medicine. He graduated as a medical doctor in 1856 but does not appear to have had any serious intention of making a career of the practice of medicine. He practised briefly near Lincoln's Inn Fields in London but soon left to become the youngest member of the Palliser Expedition. He was taken on as the expedition's natural scientist and physician.

Hector's keen interest in the natural sciences and physical fitness held him in good stead during his travels. He was also highly regarded for his wisdom, kindness, and cheerful sense of humour. "With his longer field experience, his steady judgment, and his ability to get on with the other members of the expedition and with the men,"[3] he was soon appointed Palliser's second in command. The high esteem in which the Native people held him also greatly facilitated the expedition's work.

In addition to botanical studies, Hector also made observations about the creatures he saw on his travels, but it was his geological investigations that proved to be his most outstanding contribution to science. His astonishing feats of endurance and mountaineering skill facilitated one of the most important contributions the Palliser Expedition made to the understanding of the geographical features of North America: the defining of six passes and the subsequent creation of the first accurate map of the Rocky Mountains south of Athabasca Pass.

After completing their work in western Canada, members of the Palliser Expedition continued on to the west coast and made their way back to Britain from there. While on the west coast, Hector made a geological examination of Vancouver Island and toured the gold fields of British Columbia, California, and northern Mexico.

On returning to England in 1860, Hector was awarded the gold medal of the Royal Geographical Society. In 1862 he left for New Zealand to become a geologist to the province of Otago. Three years later, he was named director of the Geological Survey of New Zealand, and in 1866 he was elected to the Fellowship of the Royal Society. Over his lifetime he wrote seventy-one scientific papers, and eleven plants in New Zealand have the name *Hectori* included in their scientific names. Over his lifetime he was given several more scientific awards and was knighted in 1887.

Hector married the daughter of Sir David Monroe in 1868. They had five children, two sons and three daughters. In 1903 Sir

Rocky Mountain explorer James Hector (r) with Captain John Palliser, the first men to enter the mountains with the sole objective of exploring. Hector explored extensively in the area south of Athabasca Pass and north of Banff.

James and his son Douglas decided to return to western Canada to revisit some of the places the aging explorer had visited during the 1857–60 trip. Unfortunately, the holiday took a tragic turn. Douglas developed acute appendicitis and died in a Revelstoke hospital. Overcome with grief, Sir James Hector returned immediately to New Zealand. He died there four years later, on August 16, 1907.

As Hector and his party made their way toward the Kootenay Plains, another mountain visitor was nearing the end of his extended hunting trip in the mountains. Also headed for the Kootenay Plains, James Carnegie, Earl of Southesk, laboriously made his way over Job Pass and down Corral Creek. He followed Hector's footsteps in reverse over Pipestone Pass, then followed what he called the Bow River Road on to the Bow Valley. Upon leaving the Pipestone River valley, Southesk noted a tree blazed: "Exploring Expedition. Aug. 23, 1859. Dr. Hector."[4] The first two non-Aboriginal men to travel in the wilds of the Front Ranges of the Rocky Mountains had missed each other by a mere ten days!

Even though Hector and Southesk had a shared interest in mountain exploration, they could not have been more different when it came to camp behaviour. Southesk maintained a strict master/servant relationship with his Native guides and other helpers and spent much time alone in his tent. As the hired help laboured to secure his comfort and well-being, Southesk found a comfortable spot to relax with a Shakespearian masterpiece. He often lamented the absence of a companion from his own class background with whom he could converse and share meals. Nevertheless, he maintained the respect of his guides and helpers, with whom he had a sound relationship.

Hector, on the other hand, wished to share fully in the life of the expedition. Unlike the tourist/explorers of the fourth period, he did not have a head guide to make arrangements and lead the group. Instead, he largely filled that role himself. He relied on the support of the Aboriginal guides he employed to lead the way and the Aboriginal hunters who nourished the party. He also hired non-Aboriginal helpers to set up camp, cook, load the pack horses, and carry out other camp and trail duties, but there was no job he did not assist with.

In the words of Peter Erasmus, a well-educated Métis guide and translator who accompanied Hector:

> Dr. Hector alone of all the men of my experience asked no
> quarter from any man among us, drivers or guides. He could
> walk, ride, or tramp snowshoes with the best of our men,

James Carnegie, Earl of Southesk, determined to find "sport" among the larger animals of the Rocky Mountains.

and never fell back on his position to soften his share of the hardships, but in fact gloried in his physical ability after a hard day's run to share in the work of preparing camp for the night, building shelters from the wind, cutting spruce boughs, or even helping get up wood for an all-night fire. He was admired and talked about by every man that travelled with him, and his fame as a traveller was a wonder and a byword among many a teepee that never saw the man.[5]

Peter Erasmus (1833–1931)

Peter Erasmus played a remarkable role in Rupert's Land's transition into western Canada. An outstanding guide and interpreter, he was an assistant to Dr. Hector of the Palliser Expedition, worked with and interpreted for missionary Rev. Thomas Woolsey, observed first-hand the events of the Riel Rebellions, and was an interpreter at Treaty No. 6. A man of many skills, he also worked as a trapper, hunter, trader, and teacher.

Peter Erasmus was born in the Red River settlement on June 27, 1833, to a Danish father and an Ojibwa mixed-blood mother. After the death of his father, sixteen-year-old Peter took over running the family farm. The work was not, however, to his liking and he did not last long as an agriculturalist.

He taught at a mission in The Pas for a while. Being a remarkable linguist who spoke Cree, Ojibwa, English, Blackfoot, and Stoney, he helped his missionary uncle translate the Bible into Cree. His work was so promising that he was sent back to Red River to study for the ministry at St. John's School. However, not feeling inclined to the ministry, he quit when the opportunity to act as assistant to the Rev. Woolsey arose. After two years guiding Woolsey and translating his sermons

to the Native congregations, Erasmus left to join Dr. Hector of the Palliser Expedition, and then spent three years assisting the McDougall family of missionaries in today's southern Alberta. In 1865 he began a new phase of his life: that of family man. He and his bride, Charlotte Jackson, settled at Whitefish Lake, south of what is now Lac La Biche. Erasmus built a house and began a life of trapping and trading, first as an independent, then for the Hudson's Bay Company. His work as interpreter for the Plains Cree in the 1876 treaty negotiations led to a position as government interpreter. He also worked as a teacher and filled various positions with the Department of Indian Affairs. The last years of his life were spent living with one or another of his six children. He died on May 28, 1931, at the age of ninety-seven. His unmarked grave in a little cemetery on a hill overlooking his first home at Whitefish Lake does not betray the legend Peter Erasmus had become, even during his own lifetime.

Peter Erasmus, guide and interpreter, also trapped, hunted, traded, and taught. He was already a legend within his own lifetime.

MOUNTAINEERS

The Pipestone Pass, which divides the waters flowing south to the Bow River from those flowing north to the North Saskatchewan, has seen a wide range of human activity. Archaeological evidence suggests that it has probably been used since very early days; the Kootenays and Stoneys knew it well. Colonialism arrived with Hector and his party, followed by the Earl of Southesk's more imposing form. It was not long before pleasure travellers made their way to the area.

The first recorded mountaineers to use Pipestone Pass and the Siffleur River as an alternative to the Bow/Mistaya River route to the North Saskatchewan were the Rev. Harry Nicholls of Chicago, the Rev. Charles Noyes of Boston, lawyer Charles S. Thompson of Illinois, and attorney George M. Weed of Boston. The foursome wanted to climb in the vicinity of Bow Summit and perhaps make a try on Mount Balfour. Tom Wilson, who supplied the outfit with Ralph Edwards as guide and packer and Wilfred Beatty as cook, felt it was necessary to give his guide special instructions for this trip: "Ralph, there's one thing you'll have to look out for. This is a mixed outfit; there are two lawyers and two clergymen, so I wish that you'd consider their feelings and be a little guarded in your remarks to the cayuses when you're on the trail."[6] (In those days, outfitters addressed their horses by cursing, although it was very unusual for anyone to curse in front of a clergyman.)

The four climbers arrived in Laggan by train the morning of July 30, 1898. They chose to spend the following day around Lake Louise while the hired men completed final preparations for the trip and set out with the pack horses and two saddle horses. The climbers began their hike the morning of August 1, managing to catch up with the pack train just before dark. Edwards soon found out what type of men he would be spending the next several days with. He later declared: "I have travelled with 'all sorts and conditions of men,' but I have never met four finer men than these into whose company I had been pitchforked. They were kind, considerate, unselfish, loyal, courteous, with not the slightest hint of the positions of employer and employee."[7]

Ralph Edwards, mountain guide and packer, got his start working for Tom Wilson.

On August 2, the pack train climbed the very steep approach to Pipestone Pass and descended into the Siffleur Valley. The trail was well defined, allowing them to make good time. They soon encountered a stream flowing into the Siffleur that was larger than the river itself. Could this be the North Saskatchewan? None had been there before. Edwards was convinced it was not, but the others wondered. Eventually they decided to explore the stream, hoping it might offer a new route to the Bow River. The faint trail soon disappeared. Before nightfall they arrived at a long narrow lake with a good camping spot and feed for the horses. Thompson named it Lake Isabella, in honour of his sister.

The next day, Edwards and Weed went ahead to see if a pass did indeed exist. They found one – a beautiful, flat alpine meadow, complete with a lake. The following day, the entire expedition traversed the pass and proceeded to discover another lake across a rocky spine. Nichols named the two lakes Katherine and Helen, after two of his daughters. He later named two other small lakes along the route Margaret, for another daughter, and Alice, after his wife. As for the pass and the creek, the rest of the party wished to name them after the leader of their expedition, but Noyes dissented. Noting geological similarities to the Tyrolean Dolomites, he successfully lobbied for the pass to be named Dolomite Pass. Late that day, they arrived at Bow Lake, two days ahead of schedule. After considerable effort and several attempts, they succeeded in climbing Mount Balfour.

In spite of its beauty, the Dolomite Pass route to Bow Summit never became popular. Aside from a hunting party Edwards took from the North Saskatchewan River up the Siffleur and over Dolomite Pass to the Bow River a few years later, there are no reports of the trail being used again prior to the 1930s.

The Pipestone Pass portion of the route, on the other hand, was used just a few days later by a mountaineering party out to conquer a giant, and perhaps restore it to its legendary greatness. In 1827 botanist David Douglas had crossed Athabasca Pass with the spring fur brigades. En route, he climbed a mountain on the north side of the pass, which he named Mount Brown and declared to be the highest known mountain on the North American continent, with an estimated height of 16,000 to 17,000 feet (4,877 to 5,182 metres). In 1893, sixty-six years later, the Coleman Brothers, Arthur and Lucius, succeeded in reaching Mount Brown and dethroned it to a height of 9,050 feet (2,758 metres), a huge disappointment for mountaineers (see Route IV on page 177).

Despite the respect Professor Coleman commanded, some mountaineers were not prepared to accept his judgment. So, in the spring of 1898, British mountaineers Norman Collie, Hugh Stutfield, and Herman Woolley set out "to reach the actual sources of the vast river systems of the Saskatchewan, the Athabasca, and the Columbia; to explore and map out the unknown mountain country where they take their rise; to locate, and perhaps to climb, the semi-fabulous peaks of that region; to rehabilitate, if the facts permitted, the outraged majesty of Mount Brown..."[8] They intended to use Hector and Southesk's route over Pipestone Pass and then travel west and north along the North Saskatchewan.

The three men left Liverpool on July 14 aboard the steamer *Labrador*. By Friday the 29th they had arrived in Banff. Two days later, they joined the American clergy and lawyers on the train to Laggan, where they met the outfit Tom Wilson had arranged. Bill Peyto was in charge, assisted by packers Nigel Vavasour and Roy Douglas and cook Bill Byers. They had a total of thirteen horses – considered an insufficient and unlucky number – and three dogs, "a most undesirable addition to a travelling outfit."[9]

A well-camouflaged marmot on top of
Dolomite Pass

Mountaineers often preferred to walk rather than ride, both because they tended not to be experienced horsemen and because they needed to get into shape for climbing after a winter of sedentary office jobs. In this case it was just as well, as all the horses were required for the baggage and the four hired men. Outfitters and their men never walked.

By noon of July 31, Collie wrote:

> The horses were packed and we were off into the wilds. ... Peak after peak, snow-clad and glacier-crowned, came into sight as we climbed higher up the thickly wooded hillside. For many weeks it would be good-bye to civilisation and its conventions and boredoms. ... The wilderness lay between us and dull Respectability; we could wear what we liked, and enjoy the ineffable delights of being as disreputable as we pleased. Out here Nature and mankind (only there was no mankind) were alike untamed: there were no game-laws, and trespassers would not be prosecuted; and, last but not least, we could burn as much wood ... and chop down as many trees as we wished without fearing the terrors of the law. To two of us the experience was a novel one, for neither Stutfield nor Woolley had ever been in the backwoods before...[10]

This glowingly positive attitude was soon put to the test. The men found part of the trail choked by dead timber. The unlucky number of horses was soon reduced to a dozen as one unfortunate beast broke a leg jumping fallen logs. The weather was hot, the mosquitoes were thick, the ground was hard for sleeping on and the food – consisting of incredibly strong

Above Opposite: Bill Peyto, one of Banff's most famous guides, was also a trapper, prospector, miner, explorer, and park warden.

Below Opposite: Dr. J. Norman Collie (l) and H.E.M. Stutfield "assisting the choppers" in clearing the trail. Paying customers did not help the hired men!

tea, doughy bannocks, fried onions and fat bacon – was indigestible. The three adventurers grew increasingly out of sorts.

"However," Collie explained "... the symptoms, if severe, were only temporary; and we had all recovered our usual health when, on the third afternoon, we pitched the tents in a pretty spot among the trees an hour below the Pipestone Pass."[11] Despite attacks by bulldog flies, they were beginning to adjust to their environment. The following morning, August 3, they proceeded over the pass and down the Siffleur to its junction with Dolomite Creek. Here, Peyto conveyed each of the mountaineers across the river on his horse. A tangled mass of fallen trees impeded their progress on the far side, requiring hours of chopping by the hired men while the paying guests sat on a log fighting off mosquitoes.

The challenging conditions led Collie to conclude that "travelling in the Canadian Rockies is far more difficult and tedious now than it was forty years ago, in the days of Hector and Palliser, when game was more abundant, and the passing to and fro of Indians and trappers kept the trails open. In these times things are altogether different; the woods are a veritable wildernesses, and, strange as it may seem, we never once met a human being – red, black, or white – during either of our journeys up country in 1898 or 1900."[12]

They would almost have doubted that the trail had ever been used, except that they observed "an occasional 'blaze' or notch cut in the bark of a tree. We also picked up an old, weather-beaten copy of Hamlet that had been dropped by some hunter or prospector; while now and then the teepee poles of old Indian camping-grounds were seen."[13] The copy of *Hamlet* had actually been left behind twenty-nine years earlier by Southesk, who was as fond of reading Shakespeare as he was of hunting.

Once Collie and his party emerged from the Siffleur Valley into the main valley of the North Saskatchewan, the trail improved considerably. They were able to proceed quickly on to the Kootenay Plains, near where the Siffleur River flows into the North Saskatchewan. The plains, also known as *Kadonnha Tinda*, or Meadow of the Winds,[14] are a unique ecological feature, a true short-grass prairie. With warmer winter temperatures and less snow than the surrounding area, they make an ideal wintering place for horses. They are also a traditional meeting place for the Aboriginal peoples of the North Saskatchewan River corridor, who gathered there to trade, dance, and feast.

Not a soul was to be found there, however, when Collie, Stutfield, and Woolley arrived. Most Natives and trappers had already deserted the area for the summer, and it had not yet become the hive of activity it was to become later in the fourth period of exploration. Unknowingly anticipating the combination horse ranch and trading post Tom Wilson was to establish in the fall of 1902, Collie named a glacier-covered mountain in full view up river from the plains Mount Wilson in his honour.

Collie and his party continued west along the North Saskatchewan River, then north into the valley of the Athabasca as they continued their search for Athabasca Pass. They did not manage to reach the pass but did have a very successful summer of climbing. Their most notable achievement was being the first Europeans to view the tremendous expanse of the Columbia Icefield, the centre of the greatest accumulation of ice in the Rocky Mountains. After six weeks in the wilderness, they returned to Laggan on September 10.

The Siffleur River viewed through a burned-out area. The large amount of deadfall after a forest fire makes passage extremely difficult.

KOOTENAY PLAINS

Between 1902 and 1908, Pipestone Pass was frequently used by Tom Wilson and his men to gain access to Wilson's horse ranch and trading post on the Kootenay Plains. The latter consisted of three sod-roofed log cabins and a corral located where Whiterabbit Creek flows into the North Saskatchewan River. Wilson hired Silas Abraham and other local Stoneys to build the four structures for him and in the first winter kept about forty horses there.[15]

Twice a year he herded his horses across Pipestone Pass, taking them to Banff in the spring and returning them to the Kootenay Plains in the fall. Occasionally, disaster struck. One fall, guide Bob Campbell started over Pipestone Pass with a herd of 171 horses. An unexpected snowstorm near the pass killed twenty-three horses and sent the remainder back to Lake Louise.[16]

Wilson himself nearly lost his life crossing Pipestone Pass in a 1908 winter storm. In his characteristic downplaying manner, Wilson says: "There is not much to tell of my trip over the Pipestone Pass. It was simply

Opposite: Tom Wilson (l) with Morley Beaver, a member of the Stoney tribe with whom Wilson traded during his winters on the Kootenay Plains.

Below: Herd of horses on the Pipestone Pass trail en route to their winter pasture at the Wilson ranch on the Kootenay Plains.

the case of a man starting on a seventy-mile [121-kilometre] snowshoe trip across the mountains to eat his Christmas dinner with his wife and family and of getting there and eating the dinner, the pleasure being well worth the trip. I rode within eight miles [12.9 kilometres] of the summit and started the next morning on snowshoes to cross the pass."[17]

Opposite the Clearwater Gap, about two miles (3.2 kilometres) north of the summit, a blizzard developed. In a whiteout, Wilson descended to the creek bottom, where he fell through a snow bridge. He found himself far above timberline with two dangerously wet feet. That night he managed to cross the pass and find enough timber for a fire. Even so, the wind was blowing so hard he could not dry his socks.

By 9:30 p.m. he gave up, put on his wet footwear and started down the valley, feeling his way along with a stick. By daylight, he was able to build another fire and finally dry out. His feet had been thawed twice already and were beginning to hurt. After consuming what food remained, he resumed the trek to Laggan. It took three days tramping with large snowshoes in soft snow. The last day he could only make fifty yards (46 metres) without resting, explaining that "the chief trouble I had was to keep from going to sleep; it would have been so much easier to quit than to go on."[18] He made it home alive but had to have portions of both feet amputated. He needed to rest nearly two years before heading out on the trail again.

Within a year of his recovery, Tom Wilson sold his ranch, his 140 head of horses, and the trading post on the Kootenay Plains to his son John and outfitter Jimmy Simpson. For the next seven years the younger Wilson and Simpson continued Wilson's established routine of loading up pack horses with trade goods and food to carry over Pipestone Pass to the Kootenay Plains cabins at the end of each outfitting season. They also continued Wilson's practice of snowshoeing across the pass to Banff in the winter. Unfortunately, Wilson's successors were not immune from the hazards that had befallen him.[19]

One fall, Jimmy Simpson and a string of fourteen pack horses got caught in a blizzard on their way over Pipestone Pass. It was all he could do to keep them on course, thwarting their desire to turn back in the whiteout. Luckily none of the packs came off and they eventually made it to the ranch, but Simpson came close to freezing to death in the process.[20] Winter storms were not the only challenges the new enterprise faced. Friction between the partners, coupled with the Wilsons' inability to secure a federal lease on the land, led to the 1918 dissolution of the partnership. Simpson eventually sold his interests to Morley rancher Frank Wellman.

Tom Wilson on snowshoes. Wilson nearly lost his life snowshoeing over Pipestone Pass in a 1908 snowstorm.

COAL EXPLORATION

A more invasive commercial use of Pipestone Pass was also taking place around the turn of the twentieth century. In 1892 surveyor R.G. McConnell's quest for coal had led him and his Stoney guides along James Hector's path over the Pipestone Pass and down the Siffleur to the North Saskatchewan River. He surveyed the valley and made a geological inventory from east of the Kootenay Plains to the mouth of the Howse River and on to Howse Pass.[21]

Tom Lusk, a heavy-drinking, short-tempered fugitive from Texas, stayed sober long enough to prove an excellent head guide for Martin Nordegg's exploration trips over Pipestone Pass and east into the foothills.

Fifteen years later, when virtually all travellers on the Rocky Mountains' historic trails were there for pleasure, Martin Nordegg made an exception of himself by following McConnell's lead. This German entrepreneur, who came to Canada in 1906 in search of investment opportunities for his German backers, channelled his hopes for commercially viable coal deposits toward the foothills of the Rocky Mountains.

To this end, Nordegg teamed up with Dr. D.B. Dowling of the Geological Survey of Canada and hired Stuart Kidd, a Morley storekeeper and ranch manager. Dowling brought his expertise in western coal exploration to the effort; Kidd would be in charge of supplies, with Tom Lusk as head packer.

In the spring of 1907, Nordegg's large pack train set out westward from Morley[22] toward the Bighorn area of the foothills. After a few days, the wagon road along the Bow River became a narrow trail, which they followed to Lake Louise and on toward Pipestone Pass.

MARTIN NORDEGG (1868–1948)

Martin Cohn was born on July 18, 1868, in a small town named Reichenbach, in what was then the Prussian province of Silesia. His father, Moritz Cohn, a Jewish rabbi, had been called there from Rawitsch, a small town in the Prussian Province of Posen, nine years previously as a preacher and teacher of religion. However, he and his wife, Auguste, gave their son a very Christian name in an attempt to avoid the anti-Semitism so prevalent at the time.

At age six, Cohn started his education in the town's Lutheran elementary school, since Jews were not allowed to attend the Catholic school and there was no Jewish school. He progressed to the *Realgymnasium*, or high school, and went on to the Technical Institute in Berlin, followed by compulsory military service. He

Martin Nordegg, ready for his first trip over Pipestone Pass.

was discharged from the military in 1894, following a fracture of his right arm that made him unsuitable for further service.

After his discharge, Cohn returned to his studies, attending the Gewerbe Institute in Berlin, studying photochemistry under the famous Professor Hermann Vogel. His association with Vogel led to a meeting with the entrepreneur Georg Buxenstein, who hired Cohn and sent him to England to work in 1896. While in England, he met and married a French woman, Berthe-Marie Brand. They had one child, Marcelle, born on July 20, 1898. In 1902 Cohn and his family returned to Berlin to manage Buxenstein's Photochemigraphical Institute.

Three years later, Buxenstein asked Cohn to entertain a Colonel Talbot who was visiting from Canada. The visitor so impressed young Cohn with Canada's tremendous opportunities for talented young men like him that Cohn decided to head west. He convinced Buxenstein to organize a company that would invest money in Canada. They called the company the Deutsches Kanada Syndikat and issued shares worth a total of $100,000. On May 3, 1906, Martin Cohn said good-bye to his wife and daughter and sailed for Canada to seek investment opportunities for his German backers. Three years later he legally changed his surname to the very unusual Nordegg. No reason for the change or for the choice of name has ever been uncovered.

The culmination of Nordegg's entrepreneurial efforts in Canada was the establishment of the Nordegg coal mine and the town of Nordegg as a place for the coal miners and managers to live. Over its lifetime of forty-two years, the mine produced ten million tons of coal.

Although Nordegg's early business life was very successful, his private life during that period was considerably less so. His wife suffered from mental disorders – undoubtedly aggravated by the fact that she seldom saw her travelling husband. She died in Switzerland in 1924. Their daughter Marcelle also suffered from mental illness in her later life and died in a sanatorium in Germany toward the end of the Second World War.

Nordegg's business success also suffered a sharp decline following the onset of the First World War. He was removed as vice-president, director, and manager of the Brazeau Collieries; then he was asked to leave Canada in 1915. Nordegg relocated to Atlantic City, New Jersey, where he met Sonia Marcelle in 1917. Soon after his first wife's death, they entered into a long and happy marriage.

The couple lived mainly in the United States during the two wars and in Canada in the period between wars. Between the wars, Nordegg also travelled widely in Europe, involving himself in a variety of business efforts. Depressed and ill toward the end of his life, Nordegg wanted to return once more from his new home in New York City to the town that bore his name. However, a planned trip to Alberta in 1948 to visit the town and the Rocky Mountains did not happen. He suffered a heart attack in February of that year and never recovered. He died in New York City on September 13, 1948, at the age of eighty.

Nordegg had eagerly anticipated his first pack-train journey through the Rocky Mountains. He approached the trip with the romantic notions of a European traveller very familiar with the Alps. However, as he approached Pipestone Pass, the terrain became increasingly challenging. Confronted by apparently insurmountable deadfall, frequent swamps, and wet weather, he quickly learned the harsh side of backcountry travel through the Rockies.

Nordegg wrote in his diary:

> The structure of the Rockies resembles that of the Dolomites. ... The Rockies appear in their bareness and solitude majestic and awe-inspiring. There are flowers in the valleys and passes, but not of vivid hues. And over them hang the towering crags and rocks. While the Alps are full of melodious sounds, the Rockies are silent. There are birds, but they are mute. The forests, mostly pines, extend up the mountains to the tree-limit – but often are burnt over and the trunks point despairingly to the firmament. For a pioneer, there is the great thrill of penetrating a region which hardly a human foot has trodden before him. ... At night, the noises are more prevailing. Wolves are howling in the distance. In a strong wind fallen trees, rubbing against each other make ghostlike noises, shrieking, squeaking. But no other sounds.[23]

After another two days of riding and a hair-raising crossing of the treacherous North Saskatchewan River, guide Tom Lusk called a halt. The party took a much-needed prolonged rest on the Kootenay Plains, as many other travellers had done before them and would continue to do after them. When they resumed travelling, however, they deviated from the route of previous Pipestone Pass travellers by heading east into the Bighorn region of the foothills, where Dowling had discovered promising coal deposits during an earlier visit. After a full summer of exploration, the party returned to Morley over Pipestone Pass in the autumn. They had discovered at least one promising coal field and had staked many claims.

Pack train crossing Pipestone Pass. Nordegg would have been accompanied by a similar pack train on his first foray into the mountains.

The following year, Pipestone Pass and the Kootenay Plains resumed their role as Nordegg's entry point to the foothills. Having hired James McEvoy, a former employee of the Geological Survey of Canada, to carry on field work in the foothills, Nordegg established his own headquarters in the Banff Springs Hotel. From there, he and the men he hired from Tom Wilson as messengers could traverse the Pipestone Pass to the Bighorn area as needed.

Marcelle Nordegg, enjoying a few days of rest while waiting to begin her trip from Nordegg to Lake Louise over Pipestone Pass.

One evening Nordegg received an urgent message to come to McEvoy's camp in the Bighorn area at once. Banff outfitter Jim Brewster had neither horses nor men to spare, but he reluctantly provided the three horses and the packer Nordegg needed to make the hurried trip across Pipestone Pass. Upon arrival, he learned that competitors had pulled up most of the claim stakes that had been placed the year before and had replaced them with their own. He and McEvoy ended up spending most of the summer restaking old claims and staking new claims to potential coal fields, returning across the pass in late summer.

Nordegg returned to his Banff Springs headquarters in the summer of 1912. By then, construction of the Nordegg mine and townsite were requiring frequent trips across Pipestone Pass. The last weeks of the summer were to be very special: Nordegg intended to introduce his fourteen-year-old daughter, Marcelle, to the country that had captured his heart. By this time, a railway had been constructed partway to the mine from the east starting at Blackfalds, halfway between Calgary and Edmonton, and going west to Rocky Mountain House. A trail traversed the foothills the remainder of the way.

But Nordegg did not simply wish to show his daughter the mine. He wanted her to experience Pipestone Pass, the route that had enabled the explorations that led to the development of the mine and town that bore his name. With Stuart Kidd, three helpers, four pack horses, and six saddle horses, the Nordeggs left the mine for the Laggan in early September. Despite bad weather, they had a pleasant trip over the pass, sustained by dreams of more comfortable accommodations at their destination.

Nordegg's report of the trip, written for his daughter, explained:

> The next morning turned out to be a very miserable one.... It was a bad one for humans and for animals... Our horses crawled as slowly as the minutes passed in this icy wind. ... May I remind you, my dear child, that even the most difficult hours pass. ... And these were really tough hours which you stood very bravely. The wind almost blew us over

the sharp ridge (8,400 feet) [2,560 metres] and we looked
down into the long valley of the Pipestone River. ... [W]e
got the last rays of sunshine directly into our faces ... the
prospect of seeing the railroad again at the end of it, ... a real
hotel ... with beds and baths ... and clean clothes! These were
probably the thoughts that passed through your little head;
they were mine too.[24]

The group camped early, with Nordegg "determined to start all the earlier
the next day. After all, I had mapped out my programme to be in Laggan
the next day and I stubbornly wanted to get my way."[25] Impatient with
the pack train's progress, he and Marcelle decided to take the lead. Despite
years of experience on the trail, Nordegg managed to get lost somewhere
between Little Pipestone Creek and Laggan, the same area in which
J. Norman Collie and his party had encountered such difficulties with
deadfall. Nordegg and his daughter encountered one obstacle after another.
Finding their way through the muskeg and windfalls before dark appeared
increasingly hopeless.

Then, just as Nordegg confronted the dreary possibility of spending
the night in the bush without tent or blankets, he heard a whistle. The
train! Encouraged by this sign of hope, he and Marcelle found their
way to the path. Before long, they could see the distant lights of Laggan
beckoning through the rapidly growing darkness. The warm baths and
soft beds of their Laggan accommodations were even more welcome after
the stresses of the day. They took the train to Banff, and after a few days
relaxing and visiting with friends, the Nordeggs continued their journey
by train to Vancouver.

By the time their train reached the coast, word had spread about their
journey. On Saturday, September 28, the *Vancouver Sun*'s morning edition
published an interview with Marcelle: "Little Miss Here From Thrilling
Trip – First Woman Over the Pipe Stem Pass."[26] Though the text clarified
that the honour being bestowed was that of the first non-Aboriginal
woman to cross the pass, even this was not the case. Mary Schäffer and
four female companions had crossed Pipestone Pass in the summer of

1906 (see page 104). Nevertheless, Marcelle was certainly the youngest non-Aboriginal woman to have crossed the pass at that time, on a journey that undoubtedly created enduring memories for both father and daughter. After some time visiting on the west coast, the two took the train back to Toronto, then travelled by ship to Genoa, Italy, where Marcelle was reunited with her mother. The three sailed together to Naples, from where mother and daughter proceeded to their home in Egypt and Nordegg returned to Alberta.

Little did Nordegg know at the time, his own days in Alberta were also numbered. One beautiful June day in 1914, he left the mine site at Nordegg and crossed Pipestone Pass to spend a few weeks visiting and relaxing in Banff. On June 28, the beginning of hostilities in Europe was announced at the hotel. Nordegg rode out to check on the mine site, knowing that many of the miners were from European countries directly affected by the conflict. All was quiet, and Nordegg returned to Banff on what was to be his last trip over Pipestone Pass.

Although he was not among the many German nationals interned in Canada, Nordegg was asked in June 1915 to leave for the then-neutral United States. Labelled an "enemy alien," he lost his position as vice-president of Brazeau Collieries, and all of his involvement with the company was curtailed. The First World War changed his world irreversibly. No longer could Martin Nordegg pursue his mining interests in the foothills of the Rockies. Toward the war's end, even his company, the Deutsches Kanada Syndikat, was dissolved. The Nordegg mine, on the other hand, was a successful commercial operation until the 1950s, when the mine closed and the town of Nordegg became a ghost town. Today, the town is being revived as a vibrant small community in the eastern foothills, with much of the original town preserved.

Adventurers

As Nordegg passed back and forth over Pipestone Pass for business purposes, others continued to use the route for pleasure. Six years before he led his daughter over the trails, a group of adventurous women had paved her way. But where Marcelle Nordegg's trip undoubtedly strengthened her bond with her father, Mary Schäffer's drew a firm line of incompatibility between her and most of her trail mates.

Mary Schäffer and her husband, Charles, had been exploring the Rocky Mountains in search of wildflowers since the early 1890s. After Charles's death in 1903, Mary's travels grew increasingly ambitious (see Route I on page 32). She began taking exploratory trips of one to two weeks' duration, stretching her abilities to withstand the rigours of horsemanship and camping. Schäffer was also trying to find compatible trail mates, so essential to successful backcountry trips.

By 1906 she was in the final experimental stages of what were to become very extensive trips. For her second trip of the summer, Schäffer, along with Mollie Adams, Henrietta Tuzo, Dorothea Sharp, and Zephine Humphrey, left Lake Louise on July 24. Outfitted by Billy Warren and Bob Campbell, they had planned a seventeen-day trip using the trail over Pipestone Pass and down the Siffleur River to visit the Stoneys on the Kootenay Plains.

The trail had seen bands of Aboriginal people pass back and forth. It had been traversed by Hector and his Stoney guides, and by Southesk and his servants. The feet of mountaineers, their guides, and their horses had trodden over it. But never had the trail seen conflict quite like that experienced on this trip. The five women soon discovered they were utterly incompatible trail mates. As Schäffer later warned: "O ye who think five women, no matter how excellent they be, can all be of one mind on the trail, take a tip from me. In three days from starting, the little woman [Mollie Adams] and I were occupying one tent while the other three had the second, I do not think one unkind word was ever uttered by any one of the five, but we had separated into oil and water."[27]

Hettie Tuzo found Mary Schäffer to be domineering and easily agitated and Mollie Adams "an enigma."[28] Meanwhile, Schäffer had found a soul-mate in Adams and complained that the other three were slow and foolish.

Never again did she travel the Rockies with a group; Mollie Adams became her regular travelling companion.[29] The two returned over Pipestone Pass to the Kootenay Plains later that summer, leaving Laggan on August 28.

The following summer, their footsteps were retraced by a group of explorers travelling from Laggan to the North Saskatchewan. A.O. Wheeler, president of the Alpine Club of Canada, had selected Arthur P. Coleman, professor of geology at the University of Toronto, and his brother, Lucius Q. Coleman, who ranched near Morley, Alberta, to perform the inaugural climb of the new club. He asked them to attempt Mount Robson, the highest known peak in Canada. Being experienced travellers in the Rocky Mountains (see Route IV on page 170) the Coleman brothers gave considerable thought to selecting the best route to their destination, which was far to the north of Laggan but west of the Continental Divide, near the source of the Fraser River.

(l–r) Mollie Adams, Mary Schäffer, and guides Billy Warren and Joe Barker in camp. Adams and Schäffer were the first non-Aboriginal women to travel and explore extensively in the Canadian Rocky Mountains.

There were three possible approaches available to them: from west of the Divide, from Edmonton, or from southern Alberta. By far the shortest was to take the train across the Continental Divide to Beavermouth on the Columbia then follow the old fur-trade route over Athabasca Pass to the Athabasca River. From there they could follow the Miette River to the top of Yellowhead Pass and down the Fraser River to Mount Robson. But Professor Coleman had attempted that route twenty years earlier and had no desire to return:

> In a straight line, Beavermouth was only 130 miles [209 kilometres] from the Grand Forks of Fraser River, but Frank Stover and I had not fallen in love with the trail when we had toiled along it with packs on our backs in the fruitless pursuit of Mount Brown. It was the shortest way in miles, but what heartbreaking miles of rock and swamp and fallen timber, not to speak of all the big rivers that had to be crossed![30]

Another possibility was to take the trail from Edmonton to Jasper, then proceed along the Miette River. This was the longest route of all and was reported to require tramping through considerable muskeg without even the redeeming presence of interesting scenery. Having dragged many a pony from the miry depths of muskeg, the Coleman brothers quickly eliminated the Edmonton route.

Southern Alberta it was. The only remaining choice was between Morley and Laggan as a starting point. The Colemans had travelled the old Stoney trail from Morley to the North Saskatchewan River and on to the Athabasca Valley many times, but the trail was falling into disuse. With the mountain sheep nearly gone, Native hunters were no longer using it and travel conditions were deteriorating accordingly.

The route from Laggan was shorter and extensively used by non-Aboriginal explorers. A well-blazed, cleared trail would lead them through

Dr. A.P. Coleman, a highly respected climber and explorer in the Rocky Mountains. He and his party did not hire outfitters, preferring to do all of the work themselves.

exceptional mountain scenery. It would also offer the Coleman brothers the added excitement of leading the first expedition from Bow Summit to Yellowhead Pass.

The Colemans did not use outfitters to convey them to their destination, nor did they employ Swiss guides. Lucius provided horses from his ranch and acquired the services of colleague Jack Boker as packer. He and Arthur also arranged for Rev. George Kinney to accompany them, as having three climbers is an advantage[31] and their previous climbing companion, Professor L.B. Stewart, was unavailable. The work of packing and unpacking the horses, setting up camp, cooking, and performing the myriad other camp chores was shared equally by the four men. No sitting on a log swatting mosquitoes while someone else did the work for these adventurers!

The six pack horses and four saddle horses journeyed from Morley to Laggan by trail, arriving on August 3. On the advice of a local outfitter, the party headed north along the Pipestone River to avoid muskeg along the

Rev. George Kinney (r), a loner who joined the Coleman brothers on their quest to reach Mount Robson. Kinney was obsessed with climbing the mountain and later succeeded with guide Curly Phillips (l).

Bow route. Had they consulted with Collie and Stutfield, they would have known better than to hope for clear sailing. Only three miles (4.8 kilometres) out, one horse got stuck in muskeg and had to be unloaded, hauled out, and repacked. Another horse got into trouble and soaked its pack fording the full Pipestone River. There was still snow on the top of Pipestone Pass, and they encountered a snowstorm along the Siffleur River.

Still, they could be comforted with the knowledge that they were not the only ones attempting these hazardous conditions. Professor Coleman, who wrote a book about their travels, explained that "at our first camp on the Siffleur a broad blaze on a tree bore an inscription proving that shortly before a party had travelled here in great state, with twenty horses, a dog, and a chef named Muy. With only ten ponies and no dog, we could only balance things by claiming four chefs."[32]

Nevertheless, it took some time for the party to settle into the routine of camp life. "Our rate of travel was slower than we had planned," Coleman explained, "and we were disgusted to find that some of the ponies were getting sore backs. We were all green to the work, and it takes some time to fall into the routine of skilful packing. 'Throwing the rope' and adjusting the 'diamond hitch' are arts so hard to learn and so easy to forget!"[33]

Six days passed before they reached the Kootenay Plains. They were fortunate to easily ford the mighty North Saskatchewan River at a braided section in order to continue their northward journey. Still, they reached the base of Mount Robson two weeks behind schedule, and as a result were unable to launch a serious attempt on the mountain. The season was late, the horses were tired, and the snow on the high passes would be getting deep. Discouraged, the party decided to return to civilization via Edmonton.

Snow on the pass was not a consideration in July of 1920, when the Pipestone Pass route was employed by a dear friend of Mary Schäffer's: Mary Vaux Walcott. As a younger woman, Mary Vaux had been a regular visitor to the Rockies, joining her brothers George and William in their glacial and photographic studies, as well as their mountaineering. Geologist and palaeontologist Charles Walcott was another regular visitor to the Canadian Rocky Mountains. After their

1914 marriage, the two travelled the Rockies together.[34] While Charles studied geological formations – constantly on the lookout for fossils – Mary spent much of her time photographing and painting wildflowers (see Route I on page 51).

In July 1920 the Walcotts followed the Bow River from Banff to Lake Louise, up the Pipestone River, and over the pass. Tending to their needs were ever faithful employee, camp manager, and cook Arthur Brown and Montana packer Joe Earle. The party proceeded along a somewhat less defined trail along the Siffleur River, which they followed until August 13.

At that point, the Walcotts returned almost to the bottom of Pipestone Pass and turned east to cross Clearwater Pass and enter the Clearwater Valley, where they spent the remainder of the month. By September 8 they were back in the Bow Valley.[35] The following summer, the Walcotts again crossed Pipestone Pass, this time heading north to the Castleguard Meadows.[36]

Caroline Hinman was another American who travelled extensively through the mountains in the early twentieth century. She was also an entrepreneur who transformed her love for travel into a business, offering Off the Beaten Track tours to wealthy teenaged girls (see Route I on page 54). In 1925 she escorted twelve guests (eleven women and one man) on an ambitious fifty-five-day outing.

Jim Boyce as guide, Bert Nichol as cook and four other packers and helpers brought thirty to thirty-five horses to carry Hinman, her twelve guests, and their gear. They began in Lake Louise, travelling up Baker Creek on July 3 and arriving at the Pipestone River on July 8. They crossed the pass that day then rested for two days before carrying on northward to Mount Robson, where they arrived on July 28. By August 27 the outfit had safely returned to Lake Louise.[37]

HUNTERS

Travellers keen on collecting scientific data and photos for their personal memory bank were not the only pleasure-seekers to cross Pipestone Pass in the early twentieth century. Those seeking the abundant game of the Clearwater and Dolomite valleys and the Glacier Lake area had also discovered the merits of Pipestone Pass. Yet, although hunting parties were a significant part of an outfitter's spring and fall business, there is unfortunately little documentation of these trips.

Mountaineer Val Fynn was one of a few hunters to record his expeditions. The account of his 1920 fall hunting trip to the Clearwater Valley was published in the *Canadian Alpine Journal*.[38] Accompanied by Swiss guide Rudolph Aemmer, with Bert McCorkell as guide and Chancy "Reno" Fitten as wrangler, Fynn entered the Pipestone River valley on August 31. Besieged by heavy rain, the group spent the night at the Little Pipestone Creek Warden Cabin.

Snow and rain dogged them as they crossed Pipestone Pass the following day, but fine weather greeted them as they set up camp farther down the Siffleur. Having missed the entrance to Clearwater Pass on the way down, they returned along the Walcotts' recent path and entered the valley on September 3. Disappointed by an unsuccessful hunt, they returned to Lake Louise on September 13, just five days after the Walcotts.

Caroline Hinman also left records of the hunting expeditions that often followed her summer Off the Beaten Track tours. In 1925 she and her friends Wiffie Lewis and Lillian Gest set off with outfitter Max Brooks and guides Bill Potts and Soapy Smith. The eleven-horse pack train left Lake Louise August 30. They camped on the Siffleur from September 1–11 before returning to Lake Louise over Pipestone Pass with a deer, two goats, and two grizzlies.[39]

Caroline Hinman's 1926 trip was perhaps more typical of her hunting expeditions in that they stayed out longer and covered more territory. She, Lillian Gest, Louise Vincent, and Hal Learned headed up the Pipestone River on August 29 with Charlie Hunter as head guide, Bert Mickel as cook, and Frank Richter and Jack La Coste as packers. The first day of hunting season was marked by cold rain, thunder, and lightning as the expedition ascended Pipestone Pass. They did not hesitate to set up camp as soon as they reached timber at the spot known as Grizzly Camp.

By September 5 the party had followed the path of Charles Noyes's 1898 climbing party into the Dolomite Valley. They continued down the Siffleur to the Wilson ranch on the Kootenay Plains, where they stayed September 6 and 7. They spent the next two weeks in the Corral Creek area north of the Kootenay Plains, returning to Lake Louise over Pipestone Pass by September 26. They claimed as trophies three goats, accredited to Learned, Vincent, and Gest. Hinman and friends again crossed Pipestone Pass and headed into the Clearwater Valley to hunt the following two years, leaving Lake Louise at the end of August and returning in late September.[40]

Hunters (l–r) Caroline Hinman, Lillian Gest, and Louise Vincent, ready for adventure on one of their fall hunting trips.

The Trail Today

The trail between Lake Louise Village and the North Saskatchewan River over Pipestone Pass is still used today. It is a fairly difficult trail and only experienced hikers should attempt it in its entirety. The first seven kilometres are an easy road and bike trail. After that, the route along the Pipestone River becomes considerably rougher and can be very muddy in wet weather. It is heavily used as a horse trail.

The route is primarily treed but opens up occasionally to provide good views, especially as you proceed north. The trail itself is often interlaced with roots, with the soil packed down in between, making for difficult hiking at times. It can also be very boggy in wet weather. One has the feeling that the trail is probably in the same condition it was in when Mary Schäffer travelled here nearly one hundred years ago – except that deadfall is now cleared from the trail. The rivers and streams are still not bridged, and the numerous crossings can be dangerous during high water.

After the first crossing of the Pipestone River, there is a good view of Molar Mountain to the west. The steep trail over Pipestone Pass then takes the hiker well above the treeline. This route affords stunning views of both the Siffleur Valley to the north and the Pipestone River valley to the south. Just before the top of the pass, there is a deep ravine on the left. This is where Tom Wilson got into trouble snowshoeing to Banff.

When I hiked the pass, there was a young buck mule deer crossing the pass via the ravine. When the deer saw me, it ran quickly away up a steep hill, true to its survival instincts, then stopped and looked to see what had startled it. I was able to "shoot" it with my camera before it continued on its way. Many a hunter has taken advantage of this trait of mule deer, with entirely different results.

From the top of the pass to the National Park boundary, the route down the Siffleur River is mainly through mature forest with fine views of the surrounding mountains. After the park boundary, the trail mostly follows an old cutline and is not maintained. There is one relatively difficult creek crossing at Porcupine Creek. The south end of the trail is overgrown and filled with deadfall, making it tough going when carrying a

Above: Mule deer on top of Pipestone Pass. This pose, which the animals strike after having been frightened and bounding away for a few metres, is a boon to hunters.

Left: South end of the Siffleur River trail showing the accumulated deadfall that makes backpacking very difficult.

twenty-three-kilogram pack. Perhaps such difficulties are representative of what the early pack trains encountered along the route. Because the route is so overgrown here, the only view is an occasional glimpse of the Siffleur River. The trail improves as you head north and gradually becomes an easy, well-maintained trail for the remainder of the trip to the North Saskatchewan River.

The entire eighty-five kilometres of the Pipestone Pass trail from Lake Louise to the Kootenay Plains has only one designated campsite. In the eighteen kilometres between the trailhead and the river crossing at Little Pipestone Creek, camping is not allowed. From there to the junction of the Clearwater Valley trail, random camping is permitted, and there are four old campsites along the route that make good stopping spots. The Siffleur Campground, the one designated campsite, is nine kilometres beyond the Clearwater trail. Random camping is again permitted near Dolomite Creek, where there is an old campsite. There is an old outfitter's camp three kilometres outside the park, but few good camping spots the remainder of the twenty-five kilometres to the North Saskatchewan River. I had to bushwhack east to the gravel flats of the Siffleur River in order to find a suitable camp.

For anyone hiking the Pipestone Pass trail from south to north, the Dolomite Pass trail provides an attractive alternative route. I describe it starting from the Bow Valley, since that is the way most people will hike it, going only as far as the top of Dolomite Pass. The trail to the top of Dolomite Pass is heavily used as a day hike. The trail begins wide and well beaten. It climbs steadily to the top of Helen Lake Summit and offers great views of the Bow Valley and its western glaciers. A few will hike the Dolomite Pass, Pipestone Pass, Pipestone River circuit, or some other combination of trails to suit their desires and/or time available.

When I hiked this route a few years ago with a friend, we had stopped by a little stream before reaching Helen Lake to have our lunch. The stream was in a small ravine that afforded good protection from the wind and was a pleasant place to rest and eat. Partway through our lunch, we heard a commotion from tourists hiking above us. We thought little of it, as the trail to Katherine Lake is a popular day hike. We expected that the hikers had spotted some marmots or other small animals and were shouting at them. After finishing our lunch, we continued on toward Helen Lake. Some of the people who had been making the commotion were still on the trail and seemed surprised to see us emerge from the small ravine. They excitedly asked if we realized that a grizzly bear had passed by just above us, running to get away from the very nervous and noisy hikers. Fortunately both we and the bear were totally unaware of each other.

I have also skied the Dolomite Pass route as far as Katherine Lake in the winter. For experienced ski mountaineers, it is possible to turn east around the lake and cross a pass into the Mosquito Creek drainage, which affords some challenging and fun-filled telemark slopes after the hard work of crossing the pass.

For summer hikers, the route from the top of Dolomite Pass to Isabella Lake is quite spectacular. The trail drops steeply through a fairly narrow valley with deep ravines and high waterfalls. Several creek crossings are required, and the trail is faint on the gravel flats in the valley bottom. However, the route is obvious and creek crossings are not difficult in periods of low water, normally from early July on.

Helen Lake from the ridge above the lake, on the approach to Katherine Lake. A friend and I were just below Helen Lake when a grizzly crossed this very open area.

Trail Guide

Distances are adapted from existing trail guides: Patton and Robinson, Potter, and Beers, and from Gem-Trek maps. Distances intermediate from those given in the sources are estimated from topographical maps and from hiking times. All distances are in kilometres.

Lake Louise to the Kootenay Plains

Maps   82 N/8 Lake Louise (Lake Louise and Yoho, Gem Trek)
              82 N/9 Hector Lake
              82 N/16 Siffleur River
              83 C/1 Whiterabbit Creek

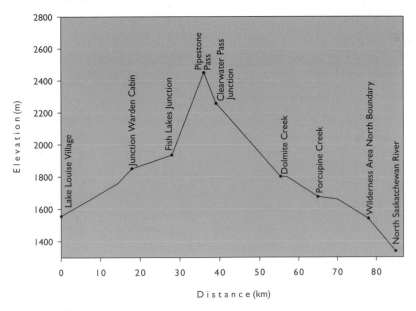

Trailhead

From the Lake Louise overpass on the Trans-Canada Highway, follow the highway west approximately 1 km to the "Pipestone" trail sign on Slate

Avenue. Follow the paved road uphill and to the left. When you reach an intersection, turn right to the trailhead parking area, following the "Pipestone" trail signs. From the north, the trail begins at the Siffleur Falls trailhead on Highway 11, 27 km east of the junction with Highway 93 and 67 km west of the village of Nordegg.

0.0	Trailhead, near a horse corral. The trail starts off on an old road and soon enters a heavily wooded area.
0.9	Mud Lake trail goes to the right. Continue straight.
3.0	First view of the Pipestone River. Continue along the edge of a high bank above the river. There are good views of the back of Whitehorn mountain.
7.0	Open area, looks like an old campground, end of bicycle access. The trail now becomes much rougher and is heavily used by horses. It can be very muddy in wet weather. The trail follows the river, with many good views of the mountains in both directions. There are several open areas that are sometimes marshy, even in dry weather.
14.5	Knee-deep ford of the Pipestone River. This is a large open section of the valley, with good views all around. The river is very braided over the next 2–3 km, and three crossings of its branches are required. The deepest was up to my knees and fast flowing but did not cause any problems. In the spring or during periods of wet weather, these crossings may be problematic. Before reaching the final crossing at the north end of the valley, there is a corral and a permanent camp used by horse parties. After the last crossing, the trail continues through the open valley, with good views.
16.0	Another old outfitter's camp. Although there are piles of tepee poles, the camp did not appear to be used.
17.5	Easy ford of the Little Pipestone Creek.
18.0	Little Pipestone Warden Cabin. The trail to the Red Deer Lakes and the Skoki Valley goes to the right. Ford the Pipestone River

(knee-deep) to the west bank in order to continue north on the Pipestone Pass trail. The trail to Molar Pass goes to the left. Continue straight ahead.

18.8   Another old campsite, complete with a pile of firewood. The trail continues along the river through a treed area, which then opens up with great views.

22.1   Continue through an open meadow. You soon come to another campsite, with a pile of tent poles.

23.4   Beginning of Singing Meadows. The beautiful meadow is open, with the river running through the middle.

26.8   Old campsite.

27.0   Another old campsite by the river. There is an easy ford of the river to the east bank.

28.0   Fish Lakes, North Molar Pass trail to the left. The Pipestone Pass trail continues ahead.

31.0   The approach to the pass is very open. One spot on the trail has pure-white sand on it. Closer to the pass, the trail was sometimes obliterated by bear diggings, which continued for some distance. The trail becomes more rugged as you climb.

35.1   The bottom of a gully from which the final rugged push to the top of the pass begins.

36.2   Stake marking the top of the pass. Moss Campion was still in full bloom in September. The top of the pass affords beautiful views.

39.2   Trail to the Clearwater Valley leads off to the right. This junction is not always obvious. Continue ahead for the trail along the Siffleur River, which is high above the valley floor.

42.7   Leave the open valley to enter the treed area.

45.7   Appears to be an old outfitter's camp. There is a trail marker carved into a tree and an old fire warning sign from the 1920s.

46.5   Abandoned warden cabin.

48.4 Siffleur Campground (Sf). From here, the trail continues along the east side of the valley.

51.6 Ford the Siffleur River to the west. This is a knee-deep crossing that did not present any problems. There is a fairly sheer rock wall on the east, very scenic.

54.3 Pass through a forested area; come to an old campsite on Dolomite Creek.

55.4 Ford Dolomite Creek. The Dolomite Pass trail branches to the left. Continue ahead for the Siffleur River trail. The creek was thigh deep and I required the use of a stick for support while fording. This crossing could be difficult in the spring. A second branch of the creek could be crossed on rocks.

57.0 National Park boundary.

60.7 Old outfitter's camp. The trail up to this point was easy to follow but had a lot of deadfall. Shortly after the old camp, a major creek comes in from the left. After crossing the creek, the trail

Abandoned warden cabin on the Siffleur River trail within Banff National Park.

is difficult to follow. By keeping to the right (east), you come to a major cutline in about five minutes which runs directly north. The cut line has been bulldozed and is partially overgrown with much deadfall. It is perfectly straight and relatively easy going.

65.0 Porcupine Creek ford. The creek is more like a set of rapids at this point, deep, fast, and full of large boulders, but the crossing was easier than it looked. Follow the cutline to the top of a hill, where it changes direction to the northeast. Continue through an area of dead trees, then cross a swampy section before coming to a point high above the Siffleur River.

70.0 Before reaching the Escarpment River, a new cutline branches to the left (north). Follow this cutline rather than continuing northeast. The trail is relatively easy going but heavily overgrown. The river is to the east. There are no good camping areas along this stretch. You may need to go off the trail down to the river flats to find a suitable camping spot. The trail continues high above the river.

76.0 Deadfall had recently been cleared from the trail. The trail turns to the northwest when it approaches the river.

78.0 Wilderness Area Boundary sign. From the top of a little hill, you get a good view over the North Saskatchewan River valley.

82.7 There is an abandoned horse corral on the right (east). The trail here is very easy.

83.8 At the bottom of a long hill, the trail turns sharply to the right. There is a sign for people travelling in the other direction, pointing to the Siffleur Wilderness Area.

85.0 Shortly after the sign, you come to the Siffleur Falls trail. Keep left on the boardwalk that continues to the footbridge over the North Saskatchewan, and shortly thereafter you reach the parking area.

Bow River over Dolomite Pass to the Siffleur River

Maps   82 N/9 Hector Lake
       82 N/16 Siffleur River
       Bow Lake and Saskatchewan Crossing (Gem Trek)

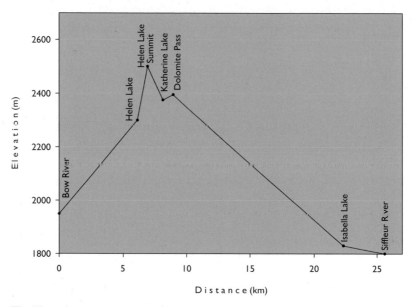

Trailhead

From the south, follow the Icefields Parkway to the vicinity of Bow Lake. The trailhead is the Helen Lake parking area opposite the Crowfoot Glacier viewpoint. From the north, hike the Siffleur River trail (above) to the junction with the Dolomite Pass trail at Dolomite Creek.

0.0   From the Helen Lake parking area, the trail climbs steadily through open forest. The wide, heavily used trail initially runs parallel to the highway and a ridge on the left, then curves to the left around the end of the ridge and continues to climb. At higher elevations, the trees become sparse and hikers can look back on good views of the Bow Valley.

6.0 Leave all tree growth behind. The trail curves around to the right (northwest) and reaches the top of a ridge. You soon come to Helen Lake nestled against the mountain.

6.9 Helen Lake Summit. At the end of the lake, the trail climbs over a high ridge overlooking Katherine Lake.

8.1 Shore of Katherine Lake. The terrain is very open. The trail continues over a slight ridge.

8.9 Top of Dolomite Pass. The top of the pass is on a flat, open meadow with no marker to indicate the top. The trail starts a gentle downhill, veering to the northwest through a well-defined ravine, then continues down into a narrow treeless valley. On both sides, mountains rise very steeply. Gravel flats often obliterate the trail, which can be picked up on the other side of the flats. The route is obvious.

12.4 Descending the treeless valley, you can see waterfalls cascading from the high ridge on the left, with deep ravines on both sides. The trail follows a ridge between the two ravines; there are views of the forest down below. You cross the stream several times, usually on rocks, and gradually make your way down to the valley floor. The scenery is spectacular.

17.0 Ford Dolomite Creek. The trail proceeds on gravel flats. It is often a good trail if sometimes indistinct. Stay on the left (west) side of the flats, entering the trees whenever it is easier going by doing so. You eventually return to a good horse trail and can follow it to Isabella Lake. The route is obvious.

22.3 Campground and warden cabin. These are on the south end of the lake. The trail follows along the lakeshore, then enters the woods at the far end of the lake.

25.2 Old campsite across the outflow stream from Isabella Lake.

25.6 Junction with the Siffleur River trail.

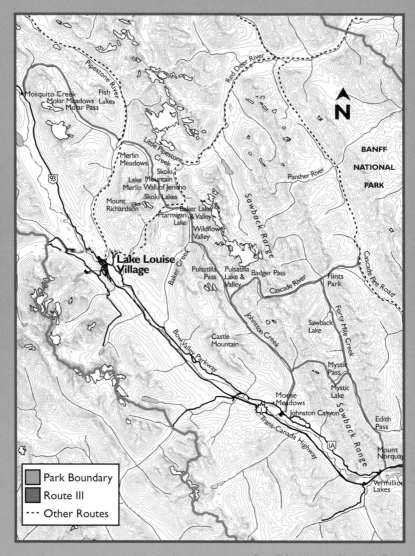

Route III from Mosquito Creek to Banff along
the Sawback Range, including Flints Park

Route III

A Feast for the Senses: Walter Wilcox and Bill Peyto's Route
from Mosquito Creek to Banff

When I was hiking over Deception Pass, heading toward Lake Louise, a mini-bus happened to drop a group off at Skiing Louise's Temple Lodge, en route to Skoki Lodge. I met the first two hikers near the top of the pass. The young women were hiking rapidly, carrying only small day packs. The only words they could muster when they saw me were, "Are we at the top yet?" I replied that they were indeed almost at the top and that by dropping down the other side they would be in the Skoki Valley and would soon arrive at the lodge. "You mean we have to climb back up here again when we leave?" they asked. I responded in the affirmative. Without another word, they departed with a look of total disgust on their faces.

Partway up the pass, I met another four hikers. They were obviously out to "do" Skoki Lodge for the weekend. They were on a mission, with an objective, a plan, a mission statement, and an execution strategy, none of which included saying hello to a bearded senior carrying a large pack. The two men were ahead and continued on their way without as much as a sideways glance. Their two female companions, a short distance behind, did manage a sideways glance and responded to my "hello" with sly half-smiles, but they continued on without a word.

Behind them, near the bottom of the pass, was an older gentleman, moving slowly but steadily. When he saw me coming, he stepped to the side of the trail and stopped. As I drew near, he greeted me and was curious to know where I had been and how long I had been on the trail. When I responded, telling him where I had been hiking, he told me he once did much the same thing, but that the best he could do for a backcountry experience now was to carry a small day pack to a lodge. He was obviously pleased that I was still able to backpack and wished me many more backpacking years. When we parted, he simply held out his hand to shake mine. No further words were exchanged or needed to be. We understood each other completely.

Chronology

1891 William Twin takes the young Brewster brothers, Bill and Jim, on a fishing trip to Mystic Lake. This is the first recorded trip along the southern end of the route.

Later in the year, J.J. McArthur takes a fishing trip to Mystic Lake, following a Native trail.

1894 A bridle path is cut along the Vermilion Lakes and as far as Edith Pass.

1894 On a trip home from Bow Lake, Bill Peyto leads Walter Wilcox on the first recorded trip along the full length of the Sawback Range. Tom Wilson had provided them with detailed instructions.

1897 Peyto repeats the trip he made in 1894 with Walter Wilcox, this time with Charles Fay, Herschel Parker, Charles Thompson, Norman Collie, and George Baker. They shorten the trip by exiting along Johnston Canyon.

1898 Tom Wilson and Jimmy Simpson lead a Virginian woman, her tubercular brother, and his personal physician on a trip over Badger Pass to Flints Park.

1910 Mystic Lake and Sawback Lake continue to be popular destinations for fishing trips, many of which are led by the Brewsters. Mary Jobe joins one of their longer trips to Baker Lake.

1911 James Foster Porter and friends explore along the Sawback Range from the Little Pipestone Creek to the Pulsatilla Valley and name many features.

1912 The Warden Service cuts a trail from Mount Edith to Sawback Lake.

Stoneys William Twin and his twin brother Joshua played an important role in the early history of Banff and Lake Louise.

1913   The Warden Service extends its trail to the Little Pipestone Creek.

1916   The Warden Service cuts a trail along Johnston Canyon.

1917   Caroline Hinman uses the newly cut trails to take her Off the Beaten Track tour along the Sawback Range to Flints Park and on to the Panther River.

1918   Charles Walcott and Mary Vaux Walcott explore the area around Sawback Lake.

1921   The Walcotts return to the area, exploring along the Sawback Range as far as Badger Pass.

1923   Leonard Leacock, Ernie Leacock, Jack Brown, Eric Stewart, and Earle Birney travel to Mystic Lake.

1926   The Trail Riders of the Canadian Rockies start at the north end of the Sawback trail and make their way along Mosquito Creek and over Molar Pass to Baker Lake, where they are met by a group that had ridden up Johnston Creek and over Pulsatilla Pass. The entire group moves on to the Ptarmigan Valley.

HISTORY

The trail that follows the Sawback Range from Banff toward Bow Lake provides a scenic alternative to the Bow Valley route. The route includes five passes as well as the picturesque Skoki, Wildflower Creek, and Pulsatilla valleys. It was these sights, rather than its usefulness in leading them to a specific destination, that constituted this route's principal appeal to early visitors. At least some of the route was an old Native trail, though it was not used by non-Aboriginal travellers until well into the fourth period of exploration.

Stoney William Twin took eleven-year-old Bill Brewster and his nine-year-old brother, Jim, on a fishing trip to Mystic Lake in 1891. They would have travelled along the Sawback Range over Edith Pass and along Forty Mile Creek.[1] The Brewster boys were probably the first non-Aboriginal people to see the lake.

Later that year, surveyor J.J. McArthur took his own fishing trip to Mystic Lake. He explained:

> Our next trip was up Forty Mile Creek. To avoid the canyon, we entered by the pass to the east of Mt. Edith [Edith Pass]. It is about 5 miles [eight kilometres] across on a good trail ... to the valley which runs in a north-west direction parallel to the Sawback Range. About 7 miles [11.3 kilometres] from the crossing, a good sized creek comes in from the west, and along this a trail leads across the Sawback Range to Johnston Creek [Mystic Pass trail] ... We made a trip to the lake [Mystic Lake] and caught two dozen trout.[2]

The good trail he followed would have resulted from traditional Native use.

Early tourist treks along the Forty Mile Creek trail resumed the following year when William Twin and the two Brewster boys escorted a Mr. Mathews on a fishing trip over Edith Pass to Sawback Lake.[3] Two years later, in 1894, the route had become popular enough that a bridle path (horse trail) was completed to Edith Pass.

Opposite: J.J. McArthur, an early surveyor and explorer in the mountains. McArthur Lake, Pass, and Creek in southern Yoho National Park are named after him.

Above: The Vermilion Lakes west of Banff have been a favourite spot since the early days of tourism in the area.

In the early days of trail development, the CPR normally cut the trails as a convenience for their guests and as a means of attracting new guests. The Edith Pass trail led from Banff's railway station along the old railway tote road that skirted the north shore of the Vermilion Lakes (today's Vermilion Lakes Road). The Vermilion Lakes have always been popular among visitors, and tourist brochures advertised the new bridle path to Edith Pass as one of the sights to see around Banff.[4]

The first complete trip along the Sawback Range from Mosquito Creek over Molar Pass, through the Skoki Valley, over Deception Pass to Baker Lake, then over Pulsatilla Pass and Mystic Pass to Forty Mile Creek, Edith Pass, and Banff, was taken by Walter Wilcox in 1895. Wilcox had just returned from Mount Assiniboine with Bill Peyto. Deeply satisfied with the guide's performance, he immediately asked outfitter Tom Wilson to arrange another trip with Peyto.

William Twin (1847–1944)

Stoney William Twin, a leader of the Wildman Band, was of invaluable assistance to easterners of the third and fourth periods of exploration in the Rockies. His traditional hunting ground was the southern drainage of the Bow River, but he was also thoroughly familiar with the mountains around the Kootenay Plains, having often wintered there with his band. It was in their traditional hunting area that young William and other Stoneys fed and befriended James Hector and his party, who had just crossed the Divide at Kicking Horse Pass and entered the Bow Valley.

In 1888 John Brewster hired William to help harvest a crop of hay for his dairy business from the marshes between the first and second Vermilion lakes. From then on, William returned every summer to help with the haying. He quickly became a friend of the family, spending considerable time with John's sons, Bill and Jim. By 1891 he was teaching the boys to hunt local big game and taking them on horseback trips into the mountains.

The small amount of English William learned at the McDougall mission in Morley stood him in good stead when development started around Lake Louise in the 1890s. He was hired by the CPR to escort guests staying at the Lake Louise Chalet around the local area. One of his famous clients was Mary Schäffer, whom Tom Wilson escorted to Lake Louise in 1893, assisted by William and his twin brother, Joshua. Though the wealthy easterners apparently did not see the absurdity in the situation, the two Stoneys, their wives, and their children had trailed horses all the way from Morley in order to provide transportation for the Schäffer party to travel the three miles (4.8 kilometres) from the railway to the lake!

William was also involved in building the first trails in the vicinity of Lake Louise. His first encounter with Walter Wilcox occurred when he was building a trail to Lake Agnes in 1894. Later that year, he guided explorers and mountaineers Samuel Allen and Walter Wilcox to the end of the lake for their attempt at Mount Victoria (aka "The Death Trap). Unfortunately, "The Death Trap" proved to be too much for the inexperienced climbers and they did not complete their climb. When the Brewster brothers set up an outfitting business in 1900, William acted as their assistant. During this time, he told John Brewster of an almost mythical land lying in the midst of the mountains three days' travel north of Banff. Eventually John went with William to see what was the Ya Ha Tinda. It was everything William had described: a meadow with good horse feed and water surrounded by picturesque mountains. The Brewsters could not resist taking a lease on the property, which they later used to winter their horses. When John Brewster died, William was reported to have said to the Brewster boys, in his limited English: "John gone. God take him. Now me your father."[5]

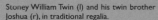

Stoney William Twin (l) and his twin brother Joshua (r), in traditional regalia.

Top: View from the top of Molar Pass, looking west across Molar Pass meadows.

Middle: Molar Pass, looking east from the ridge above the meadows.

Opposite: A view of Merlin Meadows on the approach to the Skoki Valley from the north. Wilcox and Peyto would likely have spied similar sights when they travelled the area in the early twentieth century.

mountains might be visited. This route would lead us over a course of about eighty or one hundred miles [129 or 161 kilometres] through the Slate Mountains [Slate Range] and Sawback Range, and eventually bring us to Banff.

We were to follow a certain stream that enters the Bow from the north, but as we were now, and had been for many days, outside the region covered by Dawson's map,[6] it was impossible to feel certain which stream we should take.... The second day after leaving the lake we came to a large stream [Mosquito Creek] which had not been examined hitherto.... There was no sign of a trail on either side of the stream, and none of the trees were blazed.... [A]t about two o'clock we reached a place far above timber line, – a region of open moors, absolutely treeless, – surrounded by bare mountains on every side [Molar Pass meadows].

A walk of about two miles [3.2 kilometres] across the rolling uplands of this high region brought us to the pass [Molar Pass]. It was very steep, but an old Indian trail proved that the pass was available for horses.

At the tree line a trail appeared, and led us in rapid descent to the valley. A long straight valley led us southwards for many miles.... At about one o'clock we reached the Pipestone Creek....The next day we followed up the Little Pipestone Creek. As the march of this day had brought us back to the region covered by the map, we had little apprehension of losing our way in the future. ... The next day we followed up the Little Pipestone Creek and enjoyed a fine trail through a dense forest [into Skoki Valley].

The following day, which was the first of September, we continued south over a divide [Deception Pass] and into the valley of Baker Creek, which we followed for several hours, and then took a branch stream [Wildflower Creek] which comes in from the east, and finally camped in a high valley [Pulsatilla Valley].

We were now in the Sawback Range.... [The next day we entered Johnston Creek, and] ... from this point on, we met with all sorts of difficulties.... The weather now became very bad, and we were caught near the summit of a pass [Mystic Pass] between Baker Creek and Forty-Mile Creek in a heavy snowstorm.

The descent into the valley of Forty-Mile Creek was very steep ... In some parts of the valley we found absolutely the worst traveling I have anywhere met with in the Rockies. The horses were compelled to make long detours among the dead timber, and the axe was frequently required to cut out a passage-way.... We had only found a small insignificant axe-

Opposite Above: Ptarmigan Lake and Valley from the top of Deception Pass, looking toward today's Lake Louise ski resort. Ski runs can be seen in the background on the right.

Opposite Below:The top of Mystic Pass, looking west. A very barren spot to find oneself in a snowstorm.

mark on some dead tree, about one in every quarter mile, or often none at all during hours of progress. In the afternoon we reached the summit of the Mount Edith pass, and once more caught sight of the Bow Valley and the flat meadows near Banff. A fine wide trail or bridle-path, smooth and hard, led us down toward the valley.... On the fifth of September we reached Banff late in the evening... We had been out for twenty-three days and had covered, in all, about one hundred and seventy-five miles [282 kilometres].[7]

In spite of the difficulties the Wilcox party encountered that year, Peyto repeated the trip in 1897. He had escorted climbers Charles Fay, Herschel Parker, Charles Thompson, Norman Collie, and George Baker – along with Swiss guide Peter Sarbach and cook Charlie Black – on an expedition to Mount Balfour. The Sawback Range, he decided, would make an interesting return route. However, remembering the harsh conditions he and Wilcox had encountered two years earlier, he decided to avoid Mystic Pass, Edith Pass and the trip down Forty Mile Creek by exiting along Johnston Canyon.[8]

The following year, a most unusual party journeyed along Johnston Creek and over Badger Pass to Flints Park. A young Virginian woman and her tubercular brother were out for a one-month pleasure trip. They hired Tom Wilson as guide and Jimmy Simpson – then just beginning his deep association with the mountains – as cook. The party was rounded out by a young doctor to care for the boy. On the return trip, Wilson escorted the group to Sawback Lake before crossing Edith Pass and carrying on to Banff. Unfortunately, the trip did not have its intended therapeutic value; the boy died soon after returning home.[9]

No trips along the Sawback Range were reported over the next dozen years. Yet, given the rising popularity of trout fishing at Mystic and Sawback lakes, people were undoubtedly travelling in the area. At one point in the summer of 1910, the Brewsters were reported to have led three different trips to Sawback Lake.[10] That same year, Mary Jobe, a young

Mary Jobe made her mark exploring the mountains north of Mount Robson.

teacher from Ohio who had a yearning to explore and climb mountains, joined a pack train going from Banff to Baker Lake, presumably along the Sawback Range.[11]

In 1911 James Foster Porter (see Route I on page 39) explored the Skoki Valley region, including Pulsatilla Valley – both of which lie along the Sawback trail – with a group of mountaineering friends. Porter named Pulsatilla Mountain for the Western Anemone, which blooms early in the spring.

Following up on the CPR's construction of a bridle trail to Edith Pass in 1894, the Warden Service turned its attention to cutting trails along the Sawback Range in 1912. The popularity of Sawback Lake among fishing parties led the wardens to cut a trail from Mount Edith (twenty-eight miles [forty-five kilometres]). This was followed by trails up the Little Pipestone Creek (four and a half miles [7.2 kilometres]) in 1913 and Johnston Canyon in 1916.[12] Caroline Hinman used these newly cut trails to take her Off the Beaten Track tour over Edith Pass to Flints Park and on to the Panther River in 1917.[13]

The Trail Riders of the Canadian Rockies[14] did not have the advantage of newly cut trails when some sixty individuals followed the Wilcox/Peyto route from Mosquito Creek over Molar Pass to the Pipestone River and Baker Lake by horseback in 1926. At Baker Lake, they were joined by a less ambitious group who had ridden up Johnston Creek and over Pulsatilla Pass. Together they travelled to Ptarmigan Valley for their windup "powwow."[15]

Smaller groups also continued to enjoy the beauty of the area in the years following the First World War. Geologist Charles Walcott and his wife, wildflower artist Mary Vaux Walcott, visited Sawback Lake in 1918. Three years later, they returned to explore the Sawback Range, travelling up Johnston Creek and on to Badger Pass.[16]

In 1923 Banffite Leonard Leacock, who preferred walking in the mountains to riding a horse, spent four days at Mystic Lake with his

Opposite Above: A small corral east of Flints Park along the Cascade River. Its height suggests that early wardens used it to capture elk.

Opposite Below: Looking north down into Pulsatilla Valley toward Pulsatilla Lake, from the top of the pass. Wildflower Creek Valley is just north of Pulsatilla Valley.

brother, Ernie, and friends Jack Brown, Eric Stewart, and Earle Birney (later to become one of Canada's most famous poets). They travelled to the lake on foot, with a horse to carry their gear. Starting out on the Vermilion Lakes Road, they followed a narrow trail over Edith Pass and continued up the Forty Mile Creek valley, turning left before reaching Sawback Lake. Darkness had fallen before they reached Mystic Lake.

Still, the journey to the lake was uneventful compared to the return. In spite of the lesson offered by Jack Cooley, their horse's owner, the intricacies of the diamond hitch escaped them. Leacock explained, "Every mile the pack fell off. We took turns trying and found twenty ways of tying the diamond hitch. None of them worked."[17] Years later, memories of the trip provided Birney with the setting for his poem "Bushed."

Opposite: The trail descending from Badger Pass, heading toward Johnston Creek. The larches are displaying their splendid autumn gold.

Below: Pack train crossing the steep and rugged Badger Pass. The Walcotts' pack train would have looked similar to this one.

BUSHED

He invented a rainbow but lightning struck it
shattered it into the lake-lap of a mountain
so big his mind slowed when he looked at it

Yet he built a shack on the shore
learned to roast porcupine belly and
wore the quills on his hatband

At first he was out with the dawn
whether it yellowed bright as wood-columbine
or was only a fuzzed moth in a flannel of storm
But he found the mountain was clearly alive
sent messages whizzing down every hot morning
boomed proclamations at noon and spread out
a white guard of goat
before falling asleep on its feet at sundown ...

Earle Birney[18]

Leonard Leacock (1904–1992)

Born in London in 1904, Leonard Leacock moved with his parents to Banff at the age of four. There he developed a lifelong love for hiking through the mountains. His career, however, lay not on the trails but in the concert halls. He took his first piano lessons in Boston, where he spent the war years (1914–18). The lessons were continued in Banff, Toronto, and Calgary. In 1924 he began teaching music at Calgary's Mount Royal College.

He returned to Banff each summer, deviating from the norm by hiking the trails rather than riding on horseback. He introduced many young students to the joys of mountain hiking and even ran a hiking camp at Shadow Lake in 1935 and spent a summer at Castleguard Meadows working for Pat Brewster's Banff to Jasper tours. Nevertheless, he was deeply devoted to a career in music. He taught at Mount Royal for sixty-three years, right up until his retirement at the age of eighty-three.

Leacock gave many recitals in Calgary, was a member of the Calgary Symphony Orchestra, and composed many songs and works for piano and violin. One orchestral tone poem was entitled "The Lonely Lake," perhaps inspired by one of his trips to Mystic Lake. The Leacock Theatre of Mount Royal College was dedicated in his honour in 1972. A year later he was presented with an Alberta Achievement Award for service to music, and in 1985, he was named a Member of the Order of Canada. He died in 1992 at the age of eighty-eight.

Leonard Leacock devoted his life to music but found time to hike the mountain trails and introduce young people to the joys of mountain hiking.

The Trail Today

The trail along the Sawback Range is one of the most spectacular in the Front Ranges – and indeed anywhere in the eastern Rockies. Its one-hundred-kilometre length is marked by five high passes, four of which are above the treeline and afford fabulous views from their lofty summits. Along the way, there are numerous lakes and delightful valleys. Flints Park is a flat, open bowl, surrounded by mountain peaks. It is a beautiful valley with a pleasant camping spot. The trail from Flints Park over Badger Pass is also quite sensational, as the pass is well above the treeline and affords good views down toward the Johnston Creek valley.

Despite its scenic qualities, or perhaps as a result of them, the route is not particularly easy. The passes are steep, several unbridged streams can be difficult in periods of high runoff, and sections become boggy during wet weather. The trail from Molar Pass to Skoki Valley is often reported to be a poor trail – boring, muddy, and chewed up by horses – though I did not find it to be so. The meadows at the base of Molar Pass are very attractive in the summer and make a pleasant winter camping/telemarking area in the winter. Most years a ridge of wind-blown snow builds across the meadow and enables the construction of snow caves in the hard material.

One year, I took a large group to the meadow to build snow caves and spend the night. Two young engineers, both with Ph.D.s, initially built a snow cave with a perfect dome roof, which would make it very strong. However, they got carried away and forgot their basic engineering principles. They enlarged the structure until the roof was essentially flat and soon started to sink. There was no option but to give it a strong "wump" with a shovel, which resulted in a hole about two metres in diameter in the roof. Fortunately the builders had constructed sleeping platforms along the sides and still had a roof over their heads. However, they did have the best-ventilated snow cave in the meadow!

The trail from the top of Molar Pass to the Pipestone River is generally an interesting valley trail. The trail up the Little Pipestone Creek

Trail Guide

Distances are adapted from existing trail guides: Patton and Robinson, Potter, and Beers, and from Gem-Trek maps. Distances intermediate from those given in the sources are estimated from topographical maps and from hiking times. All distances are in kilometres.

Mosquito Creek to Banff along the Sawback Range

Maps   82 N/9 Hector Lake (Bow Lake and Saskatchewan Crossing, Gem Trek)
82 O/5 Castle Mountain (Lake Louise and Yoho, Gem Trek)
82 O/4 Banff (Banff and Mount Assiniboine, Gem Trek)

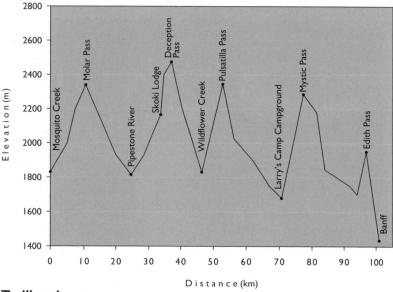

Trailhead

From the Trans-Canada Highway west of Lake Louise, take the Icefields Parkway 24 km north to the Mosquito Creek campground. A parking area is located on the west side of the road near the entrance to the Mosquito Creek hostel. The trailhead is on the east side of the highway, at the northeast corner of the Mosquito Creek bridge. From the south, take the Trans-Canada Highway west of Banff to the Bow Valley Parkway exit. Follow the parkway a short distance to the Fireside Picnic Area access road. Turn right and follow the road to the picnic area. The trail begins at the bridge that leads over the creek to the picnic area.

0.0	Trailhead kiosk.
5.0	Mosquito Creek Campground, (Mo5). The trail is a well-beaten horse path. It circles Molar Mountain – sometimes in the forest, sometimes along the creek, offering good views and bridges across side streams. There is a bridge across Mosquito Creek just beyond the campground.
6.8	Mosquito Creek crossing, bridge to the north side. As you continue along the creek, the trees become smaller and the terrain more open.
7.4	North Molar Pass/Fish Lakes trail junction, keep right (southeast) for Molar Pass. This is the beginning of a steep climb toward the pass. The trail levels out as you approach the meadows below the pass. Partway across the meadow, the trail curves left and climbs to the top of a ridge.
10.2	Top of Molar Pass meadows, a very beautiful spot. The trail continues uphill to the pass.
10.5	Top of Molar Pass. The rolling terrain on top of the pass is completely treeless, with great views back over the meadows along Molar Mountain. As you proceed you'll find that the terrain is fairly flat, with snow-capped mountains and glaciers on the right (east).
13.0	Trail begins steep descent with switchbacks. There are good views down into Molar Creek valley and you can see the creek at the bottom.
17.0	Begin descent into the valley. There are several creek crossings, none of which are bridged. Some may require fords, depending on the time of year and the amount of rainfall. The valley bottom is partially forested, with good views. You soon come to open gravel flats with more great views.
20.0	Campsite (Mo16). About two-thirds of the way down the open meadow, you ford a stream. Just across the stream is the sign for the campsite.

24.5   Pipestone River trail junction. After the campsite, the trail continues through the trees. There are some wet spots before the trail crosses over a ridge and drops down to the Pipestone River. This is the junction with the Pipestone River trail. There is an old campsite on the west side. The trail along the Sawback Range continues straight ahead up the Little Pipestone Creek. It requires an often difficult ford of the deep and fast-flowing Pipestone River. The Pipestone Warden Cabin is just across the river.

28.5   Trail junction: Skoki Valley on the right (south), the Red Deer Lakes ahead. Follow a well-beaten horse trail toward Skoki. The route is parallel to the Little Pipestone Creek. It is mainly through the woods, with some wet spots.

32.5   Merlin Meadows Campground (SK18). A good trail continues through the woods before reaching a large meadow with fantastic views. The trail stays on the north side of the Little Pipestone Creek following the edge of the meadow until it reaches the campground.

33.7   Skoki Lodge. A short hike from Merlin Meadows brings you to the historic lodge. From here it is a steady climb to the top of Deception Pass, with beautiful views of mountains, glaciers, lakes, and waterfalls to the right (west).

34.1   Trail to Jones Pass. The trail to the pass branches to the left not far beyond the lodge. Continue straight ahead.

34.7   Trail to Packer's Pass. The pass is on the right; continue straight ahead.

37.1   Top of Deception Pass.

37.7   Trail junction: to the right (south) is Boulder Pass; take the trail to Baker Lake on the left (east). From the top of the pass, proceed downhill on a good trail. The trail stays high above the creek running into Baker Lake from Ptarmigan Lake. The countryside is very open and treeless. The trail follows along the shore of Baker Lake.

40.4   Baker Lake Campsite (SK11) at the end of the lake. Just beyond the campground is a trail junction; keep right (south), continuing toward Wildflower Creek valley.

41.6 Trail junction. The trail drops down into the main north/south valley; keep right (south) at the trail junction.

46.4 Wildflower Creek Campground (Ba15). From the junction the trail goes over a little ridge, drops sharply down into the Wildflower Creek valley, and continues mainly downhill in the forest. The narrow valley gradually opens out and is quite spectacular. One kilometre after crossing the remnants of an old fence, you cross a creek via a log to reach the campground.

51.7 Pulsatilla Lake. After leaving the campground, the trail climbs steeply along a ridge. To the right is the gap where Baker Creek flows toward the Bow River. You remain in the woods for 2 km. The terrain then opens out and the trail climbs steadily to the top of a nearly treeless ridge, from where you soon reach the lake.

52.8 Top of Pulsatilla Pass. The terrain is open and the surroundings very beautiful, with great views.

56.2 Badger Pass Junction Campground (Jo29). From the top of the pass, the trail drops steeply down into the Johnston Creek valley. It remains quite open, with good views.

56.7 Badger Pass junction. The trail to the pass goes to the left (northeast); continue straight ahead. There is an old painted sign pointing toward the pass nearby, followed by what appears to be an old horse camp.

60.6 Horse camp. Just before the Johnston Creek bridge, there is a huge pile of tepee poles and a horse camp.

62.0 Johnston Creek Campground (Jo18). There is another bridge across the creek just before the campground. The rest of the trail through the Johnston Creek valley is largely in the trees, with limited views.

67.0 Johnston Creek Warden Cabin. The trail continues through the woods.

70.7 Larry's Camp Campground (Jo9). From the campground, take the trail to the left, which follows a creek toward Mystic Pass. As the trail climbs steadily, the surrounding area becomes more open. There are large rock slides higher up, with impressive avalanche paths and sheer rock walls on both sides. Near the top, the trail levels out into a very open area. The trail to Moose Meadows (see trail guide below) continues straight ahead from Jo9.

77.3   Top of Mystic Pass, marked by a cairn. The trail down the east side is steep and heavily treed.

80.9   Junction: Mystic Lake to the right (west). The trail continues straight ahead. Bridges cross the stream before and after the campground.

81.4   Mystic Valley Campground (MI22). Continue through the trees, with good views at the site of an old rock slide.

84.0   Mystic Warden Cabin.

84.1   Mystic Junction: turn right (south) toward Edith Pass, down the Forty Mile Creek trail. The trail is an old road, covered with wood chips. Its route is mostly forested, with limited views.

85.0   Junction of the horse trail, with a white painted sign.

91.8   Mount Cockscomb Campground (Fm10). Leave the road and continue on a trail.

93.2   Junction: the trail ahead (southeast) goes to Mount Norquay ski area. Turn right (south) toward Edith Pass. The trail crosses a bridge over Forty Mile Creek then climbs steadily through heavy forest.

96.1   Cross the pass in heavy forest. There is no marker at the top. The trail soon starts to drop steeply.

97.7   Junction: Cory Pass trail goes to the right (northwest). Continue straight ahead and downhill on a much more heavily used trail.

99.8   Junction: Cory Pass trail is on the right (northwest). Continue straight ahead through a very open area with aspens growing on the slopes. Just before the Cory Pass trail, a sign points to the new parking area on the right (southwest).

100.9   Fireside Picnic Area.

Connector Route from Moose Meadows to Larry's Camp Campground

Maps   82 O/4 Banff (Banff and Mount Assiniboine, Gem Trek)

82 O/5 Castle Mountain

There is very little elevation change on this route.

Trailhead

Take the IA Highway north from Banff or south from Castle Junction to the Moose Meadows parking area, west of Johnston Canyon on the north side of the road. From the east, continue hiking the Johnston Creek trail at km 70.7 rather than turning right (east) toward Mystic Pass (see trail guide above).

0.0   Moose Meadows trailhead. The route begins on an old road, which you follow. A horse trail branches off to the left (west). Later, the road splits, with a branch going to the right (east). Continue straight ahead. After this split, you join another more heavily used road.

2.7   Junction: Johnston Canyon trail comes in from the right (east). Continue on a well-packed road, first climbing steadily then dropping steeply.

5.3   Ink Pots. These waterholes consist of seven cold mineral springs at the edge of a meadow beside Johnston Creek. Water percolates up through the sand and river gravel from underground springs and remains a constant 4°C.

5.6   Bridge across Johnston Creek. The trail takes you to the east side, where a sign points to Jo9. The trail initially follows the meadow then goes right (east) over a ridge into the forest.

7.4   Larry's Camp Campground (Jo9) and bridge across Johnston Creek. Junction with the Sawback Range trail: Mystic Pass to the right (east), Pulsatilla Pass ahead (north).

Mystic Junction up Forty Mile Creek to Johnston Creek

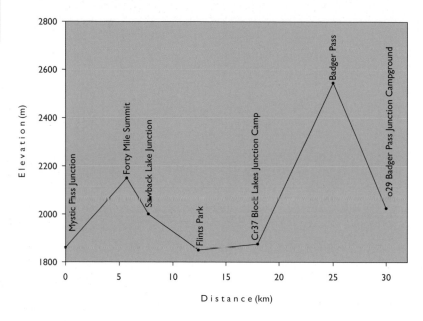

0.0   Mystic Junction, km 84.1 on the main Sawback Range trail. The trail goes straight ahead (north) from the junction and is a wide, heavily used, somewhat rooty horse trail that follows the creek through the forest. Shortly after the junction, a horse trail goes ahead; the hiker trail branches to the right (east).

5.7   Forty Mile Summit. The approach to the summit is on a single track trail through the forest that gradually thins as the summit nears. It leads downhill through an open valley, joining the horse trail before the summit. The actual summit is very open, with good views and little vegetation. Shortly after the summit, what appears to be the main trail branches to the right (east) at an unmarked junction. This is actually a horse trail to Rainbow Lake and continues on to Flints Park, bypassing Sawback Lake. Keep to the left (north) for the Sawback Lake trail.

7.7   Junction: Sawback Lake to the left (southwest). The route down Sawback Creek from Forty Mile Summit to Flints Park is a well-used horse trail with some wet sections. Sawback Lake is well worth a visit and has a campground less than 1 km from the lake (Sawback Lake, Fm29).

12.4   Junction: Flints Park and Cascade River bridge. To the right (east) is Flints Park Campground (Cr31) and the Cascade River trail to the Cascade Fire Road. Keep to the left (west), which is the trail to Badger Pass. Just after the junction a trail branches to the right, going north over North Fork Pass. Keep straight ahead for Badger Pass. The trail is an old road through a young pine forest. As you proceed west, it looks like a logged-out area, with good views.

18.0   Block Lakes Junction Camp (Cr37). Before reaching the campground, the trail heads through a meadow toward a large gap in the mountains. A white painted sign points north to Badger Lake, although there is no trail. Another sign points south to the Block Lakes and Cr37. Continue straight ahead.

19.6   Old National Parks Fire Warning sign. This sign is a remnant from the early twentieth century. The trail is fairly open and climbs steadily.

21.0   Steep climb with switchbacks begins. You are close to the treeline at this point and will soon come to a small bowl at the base of the pass. The last part of the climb is barren.

25.0   Badger Pass. As you start down from the pass toward the Johnston Creek valley, you enter a larch forest. (The fall colours are lovely by mid-September.) The trail continues through forest and an open meadow.

30.0   Badger Pass Junction Campground (Jo29), km 56.7 on the main Sawback Range trail.

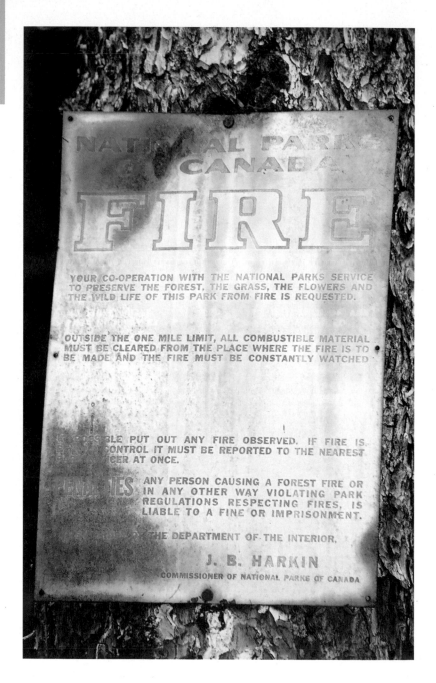

Connector Route from Flints Park
to the Cascade Fire Road

There is very little elevation change on this route.

0.0   Flints Park Junction, km 12.4 on the trail from Mystic Junction up
        Forty Mile Creek to Johnston Creek (see above).

0.3   North Cascade River bridge. The trail is an old road, heavily used
        by horses. It passes through a gap between two large mountains
        of the Vermilion Range. The one on the left is named Flints Peak.
        The trail stays just above the Cascade River.

1.7   Small, sturdily built corral about 10 ft (3 m) high beside the trail.

2.9   An old loggers brow, used to load logs on sleds or wagons.

4.0   Major horse trail comes in from the south and joins the present
        one. The area is open, with great views. As you go along, many
        horse trails cut back and forth across the main trail.

7.5   Cuthead Creek bridge. Just before the bridge, the remains of an
        old fence can be seen beside the trail.

7.8   Cascade Fire Road, km 23.1 on the Cascade Fire Road, Route IV
        trail guide (see page 190).

National Parks fire warning sign, erected in
the early twentieth century. These reflected
the early mandate of the wardens to prevent
fires and were never removed. Many are
still visible, and some remain in excellent
condition a century after being put up.

Above: A typical Caroline Hinman Off the Beaten Track group on an unidentified mountain pass.

Below: An early snowfall blankets the trail heading toward Divide Pass from the Red Deer River.

CHRONOLOGY

...1880s   Prior to the 1880s, the area north of the Red Deer River is used extensively by the Stoney people for hunting.

1880s   Tom Wilson joins the Stoneys on some of their travels between the Red Deer and North Saskatchewan rivers.

1884 or   Dr. George M. Dawson travels up the Cascade River and on (along
1885   today's Cascade Fire Road) to the Red Deer River, then turns west.

1892   Arthur Coleman, Lucius Coleman, and three companions (with the assistance of two Stoney guides) follow old Stoney trails between the Red Deer and North Saskatchewan rivers en route to Athabasca Pass.

1893   The Colemans, L.B. Stewart, and Frank Sibbald resume the quest for Athabasca Pass. They follow the previous year's route to the Kootenay Plains, accompanied by Chief Jonas.

1902   Arthur Coleman and Proctor Burwash join Lucius and Ella Coleman to retrace the trail to the Kootenay Plains. They spend most of their time exploring the Brazeau Lake area.

1912   The Warden Service cuts a trail along Dawson's route from Lake Minnewanka to Cuthead Creek.

1917   Caroline Hinman uses part of the trail from Lake Minnewanka to the Red Deer River, taking her Off the Beaten Track tour from the Panther River to the Red Deer River.

1924   Caroline Hinman and her Off the Beaten Track tour make the first recorded trip from the Kootenay Plains to Lake Minnewanka. About two weeks later, Charles Walcott and Mary Vaux Walcott travel along today's Cascade Fire Road from the Panther River north to the Red Deer River.

1930s   Today's Cascade Fire Road is bulldozed from Lake Minnewanka north to the Red Deer River, then east out of the mountains.

1988   Cascade Fire Road is closed to all vehicular traffic. Most bridges and culverts are removed shortly thereafter.

HISTORY

THE ENTIRE ROUTE

The first recorded party to travel the entire distance from the North Saskatchewan River to Lake Minnewanka via Divide Pass and the Cascade River would also have been a sight to behold. Caroline Hinman's Off the Beaten Track tour groups tended to be large, and this one was no exception. She was joined by her friend Lillian Gest, sixteen other paying customers, head guide Jim Boyce, and five helpers. They would have needed twenty-four saddle horses and at least ten pack horses.

The expedition departed from Emerald Lake in Yoho National Park on July 7, 1924. One month later, after having visited the Castleguard Meadows, the group arrived at the old Wilson ranch on the Kootenay Plains. They rested two days before starting the trip to Lake Minnewanka by following Whiterabbit Creek to the headwaters of the Ram River, then over Indianhead Pass to the Clearwater River. They continued up Peters Creek and over Divide Pass to the Red Deer River, where they arrived on August 14.[1]

The trip from the North Saskatchewan River to the Red Deer River would have followed old Stoney trails, as this area was a traditional hunting ground (see the Coleman trip on pages 170–173).[2] Near Divide Summit the party was greeted by two of Boyce's men who had come to deliver mail. "There was always an air of excitement about these meetings," Gest later explained, "and mail was an excitement in itself. We felt very far from the outside world and we really were most of the time."[3]

They followed Snow Creek over Snow Creek Summit to Harrison Creek, where they had a three-day layover from August 15 to 18. Travel along Wigmore Creek and Cuthead Creek brought them to the Cascade River, which they followed to Lake Minnewanka on August 21 and on to the Alpine Clubhouse in Banff the following day. The entire journey took approximately six weeks. There is no other record of anyone travelling this entire route prior to 1930.

Lillian Gest, a friend who accompanied Caroline Hinman on many of her backcountry excursions, spent every summer from 1921 to 1984 in the Canadian Rockies.

The Northern Half, from the Red Deer to the North Saskatchewan River

While Hinman's party is the first known to have followed the entire route, its northern half had been well travelled for centuries. With traditional hunting grounds between the Red Deer and North Saskatchewan rivers, the Stoneys knew every valley and mountain pass intimately. Their trails were well established and heavily used. They travelled along the foothills, entering the mountains through the Red Deer River gap, as did David Thompson in 1800 (see Route I on page 24). After journeying west to Snow Creek (Scotch Camp), they turned north along Divide Creek toward rich hunting territory.

This route was heavily used during the first period of exploration and saw continued use by Native bands. Being a north/south route through the front ranges, however, it was not of interest to the explorers of the second and third periods. They were mainly interested in east/west routes through the mountains.

Outfitter Tom Wilson likely heralded the fourth period of exploration in this area. Wilson, who travelled widely in the mountains, but did not record most of his adventures, is reported to have travelled to the Kootenay Plains along the Bow River with a band of Stoneys in the 1880s.[4] They left the Kootenay Plains via Whiterabbit Creek and crossed Indianhead Pass into the Ram River drainage, then over Divide Summit to the Red Deer River and east along the foothills to Morley. The inclusion of non-Aboriginal men like Tom Wilson on such journeys meant that future outfitters would be able to gain invaluable information on possible passageways through little-known valleys and passes. With Wilson's nearly photographic memory for any trip he took in the mountains, he was ideally suited for such reconnaissance.

Still, most non-Aboriginals who followed Stoney trails through the Front Ranges to the Kootenay Plains went straight to the source for their route information. The Coleman Brothers, figuring that "one alone among

Outfitter Tom Wilson travelled widely in the mountains. His nearly photographic memory made him an encyclopedia of knowledge for later travellers.

white men was sure to get homesick and desert,"[5] hired two Stoney guides: Jimmy Jacob, who spoke Cree and some English, and Mark Two-Young-Men, a young lad "who spoke nothing which any of us could understand, but had a graceful and extensive command of the sign language."[6] In preparation for a two month trip, the Colemans also purchased thirteen cayuses from the Stoneys.

Arthur Philemon Coleman, professor of geology at the University of Toronto, was intrigued by the controversy David Douglas initiated when he reported that mountains on either side of Athabasca Pass (Mounts Hooker and Brown) rose to the towering heights of 17,000 feet (5,182 metres) (see Route II on page 84). Though hopeful, mountaineers were skeptical that such giants could exist. Coleman was determined to find out for himself. He first attempted to canoe down the Columbia River to Athabasca Pass in 1884. Thwarted, he determined he would have to travel overland with cayuses. He set about organizing a far more ambitious Mount Brown expedition for the summer of 1892. The party would consist of his brother, L.Q. Coleman, a Morley rancher;[7] L.B. Stewart, professor of surveying at the University of Toronto; Dr. Laird of Winnipeg; Mr. Pruyn, an avid sportsman; and their two Stoney guides, Jimmy Jacob and Mark Two-Young-Men.

The group assembled on July 6 at the Coleman ranch near Morley. By early evening, everything was packed and ready to go. They headed a short distance north into the foothills and camped on the far side of the Ghost River. In the morning, they followed a well-beaten Stoney trail along the foothills. Because the area had never been mapped, Stewart walked the entire distance using his pedometer to measure distances, sketching the hills and streams as he went along. The journey wasn't much easier for those who were riding. "There was trouble in the muskegs and fallen timber," Professor Coleman later explained, "and every one was disillusioned and disgusted and wondered why he had come into a world of so much tribulation and such poor scenery."[8]

After enduring five days in the foothills, they turned west along the Red Deer River, following David Thompson's footsteps of some ninety-two years earlier (see Route I on page 31). By this point, everyone had

Professor A.P. Coleman, who solved the
"David Douglas Controversy."

The following year, the Coleman brothers resumed their quest for Athabasca Pass. Professor L.B. Stewart rejoined them, along with a young Morley rancher, Frank Sibbald,[12] as packer and handyman. Sibbald had learned the Cree and Stoney languages from childhood playmates, who had given him the Stoney name Tokun ("the Fox") in recognition of his hunting and tracking skills. His ability to communicate with any Native people they met on the trail was a valuable asset. The Colemans also found that he "was not only an excellent horseman and as skilful in tracking a strayed pony as an Indian, but a very fair camp cook; and his uniform readiness and good-humour added much to the comfort of a journey in which every side of a man's character and physique is often sorely tried."[13]

Having found Jimmy Jacob and Mark Two-Young-Men to be of little use except on their own familiar ground, which Stewart had mapped and with which the Coleman brothers were now quite familiar, they decided against taking guides. They did, however, pack a folding canvas boat for crossing the major rivers. Though it worked well for its intended purpose, it proved to be a real nuisance to pack on a horse – especially since the reduced size of the party allowed them to take only eight horses.

The party set out on July 8 accompanied by Chief Jonas, of the Stoney band, and his family, who were travelling in the same direction. Jonas kindly shared his knowledge of the area, drawing a map and sharing the Stoney names for some of the rivers on Stewart's map. Though directions and distances on the map were vague, it later proved to be an invaluable tool.

The Coleman party set out along the previous year's route, passing from the foothills into the mountains along the lower end of the Red Deer valley. They turned north from the Red Deer River and followed the same Native trail into the Clearwater Valley, then proceeded north down the Whiterabbit Creek to Kootenay Plains. They found that:

> the route north from the Clearwater had been appreciably
> lengthened since last summer by the fall of dead trees where
> fire had run. On an Indian trail trees are seldom chopped.

Instead, the man who rides ahead pulls his horse into the bushes when he comes to a newly fallen trunk and goes round the end of it; the others follow automatically and the trail has been lengthened by one or two hundred feet [thirty or sixty metres].[14]

The Saskatchewan River afforded the opportunity to test the usefulness of their canvas boat. After assembly, it was:

a frail enough looking punt, 12 feet [3.7 metres] long and 5 feet [1.5 metres] wide, to cross the brown river, 150 yards [137 metres] wide, which surged past just beyond the eddy. I did not like the looks of it, but Stewart, our most experienced oarsman, got in with a load of flour and saddles and pulled away manfully. The boat was swept far down stream, but landed safely, was unloaded and towed well above our camp, and came back light, swirling into the eddy at its lowest point.[15]

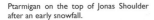

Ptarmigan on the top of Jonas Shoulder after an early snowfall.

It took several trips but they did manage to ferry their goods across the river. They then followed the Cline River to Cataract Creek, crossed Cataract Pass to the Brazeau River, and followed Jonas Creek to the Sunwapta River. From the Sunwapta, they found the Whirlpool River, which they followed to Athabasca Pass.

Stewart put the canvas boat to another use on the return journey: he parted ways with his friends at the Kootenay Plains and journeyed to Edmonton by boat. Sorry to part from Stewart, the most trustworthy, active, and cheerful of fellow travellers, and a man of cool nerve in emergencies,[16] the Colemans "apportioned to him his share of the dwindling supplies, and bade him goodbye with some anxiety as to his trip down the rapids and swift currents to Edmonton. He had 250 miles [402 kilometres] of river before him, and the little 12-foot [3.7-metre] craft with its dingy green canvas looked very frail for such a journey."[17] They were relieved later to discover that all had gone well.

Meanwhile, the two brothers and Frank Sibbald had their own adventure to face as they retraced their steps to Morley. Finding themselves short of food, they resorted to a forced march to the Clearwater River and on to the Red Deer River and Mountain Park (Ya Ha Tinda). There they found a group of tepees, heralding the start of a Stoney hunting expedition. The Coleman party's hunger pushed them on to Morley, where they arrived the next evening. They had covered the 220 miles (354 kilometres) from Fortress Lake in just ten days – very fast travel on mountain trails.

Their triumph was darkened, however, with the discovery of the Beaver family's sad news. John Beaver, who had travelled with the Coleman party for part of their previous summer's trip, had died of consumption. Coleman explained that John's father, Job, "was inconsolable, and the white men of the region say committed suicide

The Sampson Beaver family (l–r): Leah, Frances Louise, and Sampson. Sampson was reputed to be one of the best Stoney hunters of his time, and he knew the area north of the Red Deer River intimately.

in this grief, while the Indians hint that Job was not right in his head before he died. Handsome young Samson, who had visited us with Mark Two-Young-Men, was now the head of the family."[18]

Having found the supposed giants, Mounts Brown and Hooker, and dethroned them to mere ordinary mountains in 1893, nine long years passed before A.P. Coleman was able to leave his commitments in the east and return to the mountains, this time simply to do some exploring:

> My thoughts during summer heats in the east had often run longingly to the high slopes above timberline where snowbanks were just melting and the spring flowers of July were hustling one another in the race to get their blossoms open first. … To think of 80 or 90 degrees in the shade in a starched shirt, when one could be on a bare mountain top looking over a thousand square miles [1,609 square kilometres] of rock, snow, and ice, and green, dusky valleys, with a clean wind sweeping past from the snowfields![19]

In 1902 Coleman and Proctor Burwash, a friend from the east, journeyed westward to join Coleman's ranching brother and his brother's wife. They planned to use their old route to the Kootenay Plains, then extend their explorations northward. Though the route was longer than the more common trail from Laggan to the plains, the Colemans felt the effort was rewarded by "a drier climate and better beaten trails, a greater variety of scenery, and often picturesque meetings with the Indians following up the mountain sheep in the summer."[20] They arrived at the Kootenay Plains to happily find fifteen lodges of Stoneys camped. They met up with their former guide, Jimmy Jacob, and Sampson Beaver, now a married man with a family, who showed them the best ford of the North Saskatchewan River.

On leaving the Plains, the Coleman party did some exploring along the Cline River and McDonald Creek and crossed a pass to Brazeau Lake. They returned to the Kootenay Plains over the familiar Cataract Pass route, which they found easier than the pass at the head of McDonald Creek. The remainder of the trip home was along the now familiar route between the North Saskatchewan River and the Red Deer River, exiting the mountains as before through the Red Deer River gap.

They arrived at Morley on the last day of August 1902, after covering about 250 miles (402 kilometres) of rough trail without guide or packer.

> The lady of the party had shirked none of the hardships of the journey, and had effected a marked improvement on our camp diet ... but the real gain [of the journey] was the filling of our lungs with mountain air, besides renewing our acquaintance with mountain trails, those capricious, tantalising, exasperating, and yet wholly seductive pathways, leading through bogs and fallen timber nowhere, and yet opening out the sublime things of the world and giving many an unforeseen glimpse of Nature hard at work constructing a world.[21]

No other travellers recorded journeys along the northern half of the route prior to the 1930s.

The Southern Half, from Lake Minnewanka to the Red Deer River

The southern half of the route saw even less traffic. Not a single pleasure trip was recorded along just the southern half prior to the 1930s, although there was one scientific trip along the whole route and another that ventured into portions of it. Dr. George M. Dawson, pioneer geologist with the Geological Survey of Canada, travelled up the Cascade River from Lake Minnewanka to the Red Deer River in 1884 or 1885, most likely along an old Native trail.[22] Then, early in the twentieth century, the Warden Service established a trail from which to patrol the area. In 1912 twenty-seven miles (forty-three kilometres) of trail were cut along Dawson's route from Lake Minnewanka to Cuthead Creek,[23] approximately halfway to the Red Deer River. In 1917 Caroline Hinman used part of the trail on her first major trip to the Rockies (see Route I on page 54) when she followed Snow Creek from the Panther River to the Red Deer River.

In 1924 Charles Walcott and his wife, Mary Vaux Walcott, missed another Off the Beaten Track tour by about two weeks. The Walcotts were on one of their wide-ranging tours, studying geology and painting wildflowers. In late August, they moved camp from the Baker Lake area (see Route I on page 49) to Scotch Camp at the junction of Snow Creek and the Red Deer River, arriving on August 31. The large Hinman party had been there on August 14, and their earlier presence must have been very obvious to the Walcotts. The Walcott party exited the mountains to the east, travelled south to the Panther River, then followed it back into the mountains. On September 10, they set up camp on Wigmore Creek, near the outflow from Harrison Lake. Their explorations of the area included a visit to the lake. By September 16, they had crossed Snow Creek Summit and were on their way down the Red Deer River.

Travels along the upper Cascade River were simplified after a fire blazed through the area in 1936. As part of the firefighting effort, a cat-track was bulldozed from Banff to Flints Park on the Cascade River. By the late 1930s the road, upgraded and extended to the Red Deer River and east through Ya Ha Tinda Ranch, had become known as the Cascade Fire Road. It was used regularly by Parks vehicles until 1984, when it was allowed to revert to a foot trail. By 1988 all fire roads in the park were closed to vehicular traffic. Most bridges and culverts were removed in 1990. Today the southern end of the trail is used to access other hiking trails in the eastern Front Ranges and is a popular winter ski trail.

The old Cascade Fire Road north of Wigmore Summit, which has reverted to a hiking trail.

The Trail Today

The trail from Banff to the North Saskatchewan River along the Cascade Fire Road/Whiterabbit Creek route in some ways parallels the combined Sawback Range/Pipestone Pass trails as a route between the Bow and Saskatchewan rivers. The more easterly route has four passes: two before the Red Deer River, one between the Red Deer and the Clearwater rivers, and one between the latter and the North Saskatchewan River. The passes are of similar height to the ones on the Sawback/Pipestone route but are not as dramatic in terms of the steepness of the trail or the views from the top. The approach to both Wigmore Summit and Snow Creek Summit are gradual and the passes are broad, flat valleys with little indication that you are actually on a summit. Divide Summit and Whiterabbit Pass require more effort from the hiker and offer pleasant but not spectacular views from the top.

Starting from Lake Minnewanka, the old Cascade Fire Road is like any country gravel road – wide, flat, and boring hiking – until you reach the turnoff to Flints Park. Though the Cascade valley offers pleasant scenery, most hikers do not enjoy hiking on a road and will not appreciate this section of the trail. Its one saving grace is perhaps the pleasant challenge of attempting

Remains of the old corral and loading chute for elk on the Cascade Fire Road.

to deduce how the old elk corrals along the route functioned. The main corral and loading chutes are still standing, dating from the days when Parks instituted a program of elk capture and shipping to decrease numbers in the area in the mid-twentieth century. This is a protected cultural resource site.

Beyond the Flints Park exit, grasses and some shrubs have grown over the old road, making it much more pleasing as a hiking trail. After a short distance, a sign marks the site of Cuthead College. This was originally the site of a warden cabin, which became a Second World War work camp for conscientious objectors. Between 1954 and 1960, the first school for training wardens was held here. Only the sign is now left. To the north of the Red Deer River, the Divide Creek Valley – home to the Divide Warden Cabin – is beautiful and quiet, and the approach to the pass provides good views.

Just before reaching the Clearwater River when travelling north on the Peters Creek trail, there is a large outfitter's camp at the head of a meadow, and the authors have used this camp on more than one occasion. I stayed there on my last foray into the region and, as on previous trips, there was no one else there. However, the next morning, there was a curious sound coming from the river area, which sounded like the high-pitched voice of a young woman. Not expecting there to be anyone else around, especially on the gravel flats of the river, I dismissed the sound as probably being a raven or magpie.

After fording the river, I was putting my boots back on when I heard the definite sound of voices. After starting down the trail, I soon came across the camp of a group of young people. This was an organized group with local leaders and participants from across Canada. I asked them why they were camped on the river flats where there was no safe place to store their food when there was a nice camp just a short distance away. They told me they had been to the camp two days before and an outfitter was there with a helper. He told them he had a large group coming and they could not stay there.

Not wishing to cause problems they moved on. When they could not find a satisfactory place to camp, they ended up on the river flats and cached all their food on a small island in the river, covering it over with a tarp held down with rocks. They realized that a mature grizzly could remove the rocks in a matter of seconds but felt this was the best they could do. The outfitter left the next day, and his "large party" did not arrive. He simply did not want this group of very responsible young people camping in the same spot. His very short-sighted and selfish action put this group in considerable danger, but fortunately no bears came to visit. The leaders assured me they would be reporting the incident to the Warden Service. One can only hope that this irresponsible outfitter had his licence suspended.

The Clearwater Valley is one of the most remote in Banff Park and part of the trail is actually outside the park. This is a peaceful, gently beautiful valley, well worth the effort of reaching it. Whiterabbit Pass is also worth the climb, but the Ram River valley is very disappointing for a backcountry hiker.

There were a large number of motorized vehicles travelling along the Ram River (actually in the river) while I was passing through. My first thought was that they could give me passage across the river to avoid a ford. However, when I reached the river, there was not a vehicle in sight. It was only after I had removed my boots, forded the river and was putting my boots back on that they reappeared. I had to move in order to let them cross, as I was using the edge of their deep ruts as a convenient place to sit. The drivers were very pleasant and friendly and wanted to know where my vehicle was. It was inconceivable to them that someone could actually walk into the valley. Fortunately, the motorized vehicles' rude assault to the senses was later softened by the pleasant sight of a family and their pack horses – followed by a teenaged boy valiantly trying to keep up on his bicycle – who passed by the Headwaters Cabin while I was there.

This cabin was built in 1914 to provide shelter to forestry officers on patrol. Two years later, the roof was covered with steel shingles. The combination of steel shingles and fire-killed logs, which are more resistant to rot than freshly felled trees, have kept the cabin in remarkably good condition. Unfortunately, the surrounding land is now totally chewed up by quads and the inside of the cabin has been taken over by mice.

Top: A family with pack horses heading for the horse camp farther down the Ram River valley.

Above: Headwaters Cabin, built in 1914 of fire-killed logs and fitted with a steel roof, two features that have contributed to its survival.

Still, since it was raining heavily when I arrived, I decided to spend the night. Before heading to bed, I perused the cabin's log book. It had been signed by hundreds of visitors, but I could not find another person who had hiked into the area. All had come by quad and most were hunters. I proceeded to spread my sleeping bag on an old bunk bed, hoping for a peaceful night, only to have the unnerving experience of mice running across my face as I attempted to sleep!

The trail from the Ram River to the Kootenay Plains is a good, well-used horse trail that had recently been cleared of deadfall. The trail is mainly in the woods but does offer some views. The entire trail from Banff is a very peaceful backcountry hike with lots of solitude, except in the river valleys. I met horse, hiking, and quad (OHV) parties in the Red Deer, Clearwater and Ram River valleys.

The portion of the route along the Cascade Fire Road is intersected at Stony Creek, Flints Park, the Panther River, and the Red Deer River by trails that serve as entrance and exit points for portions of the trail. Beyond the Red Deer, the only entrance/exit point is the Clearwater River. Most of the route in the National Park is designated as a random camp area. I did not encounter any difficulty in finding good camp spots with the requisite water and food storage. There are old outfitter camps along the entire route and two designated campsites on the south end, on the Cascade River.

There are many unbridged streams along the route, many of which can be navigated by hopping across on rocks or by easy fords. The Panther and Clearwater rivers are major fords. They can be crossed safely with due care, but should not be taken lightly.

The Red Deer River would also be a major ford, except that a substantial steel bridge spans the water, a leftover from the Cascade Fire Road. There are major outfitter camps at this junction of trails, and the night I spent at Scotch Camp, an old outfitter's camp on the Red Deer River, was a memorable one. As I approached the camp, I saw two women watering horses at the side of the trail. They turned out to be mother and daughter, and the mother immediately asked if I had seen any horses on my trek. Hailing from a farm/ranch in the eastern foothills, she and her four teenaged children – two girls and two boys – had trailed in from Ya Ha Tinda Ranch with five saddle horses and two pack horses for their annual backcountry trip.

Their normal routine was to let three horses graze while keeping the other four tied up. That morning they had decided to reverse the process, and the four grazing horses departed for places unknown. It took an hour for the family to notice that the horses were gone, at which time the oldest sibling, a nineteen-year-old girl, saddled the strongest of the remaining horses and headed back toward the Ya Ha Tinda in hopes that the stray horses were following their homing instinct.

It was a cloudy day, with light intermittent rain. The young woman was wearing only jeans and a T-shirt covered by a full-length rain slicker. She had been gone about eight hours, and her mother was getting worried. With the family camped in the old outfitter's camp, I located myself a few hundred metres away, near the river. As I set up camp, the two boys brought some firewood and invited me to join their evening campfire.

While eating my supper, I heard the distinctive clomp-clomp of horses on the river bridge. I looked up to see a rider with three horses tied behind her saddle and a fourth horse running free close behind. She told me she had journeyed all the way to the Ya Ha Tinda Ranch gates, where she found her horses milling about. On the way, she had stopped to look at Melcher's Ranch. By this time, she was wet and cold and hungry, but, of course, the gentleman who left coffee on his deck for passing travellers (see Route 1 on page 19), took her in, gave her warm dry clothes, and fed her before seeing her on her way.

I spent a most enjoyable evening at the family's campfire. The four children wanted to know all about me. What was especially notable was that when the younger children wanted to tell a story or ask a question, the older ones patiently waited for them to finish, without interrupting. I usually find talking to a group of teenagers difficult, as they tend to talk their own language and be reserved around strange adults but not this group. The parents had obviously done a great job with this foursome, and I would like to think that their annual wilderness foray has had an important impact on these well-rounded young people, just as Caroline Hinman's tours did so many years ago.

Trail Guide

Distances are adapted from existing trail guides: Patton and Robinson, Potter, and Beers, and from Gem-Trek maps. Distances intermediate from those given in the sources are estimated from topographical maps and from hiking times. All distances are in kilometres.

Lake Minnewanka to the Kootenay Plains

Maps   82 O/4 Banff (Banff and Mount Assiniboine, Gem Trek)
           82 O/5 Castle Mountain
           82 O/12 Barrier Mountain
           82 O/13 Forbidden Creek
           82 N/16 Siffleur River
           83 C/1 Whiterabbit Creek

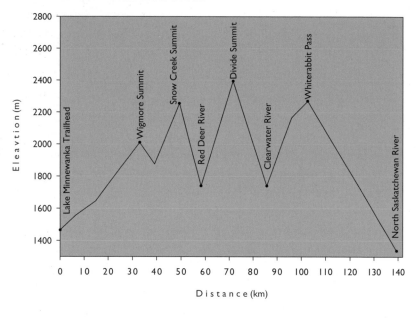

Trailhead

From the south, the trail begins at the northwest corner of the Upper Bankhead Picnic Area, located on the west side of the Lake Minnewanka Road, 3.5 km from the Trans-Canada Highway at the Banff east exit. From the north, the trail begins at the Siffleur Falls trailhead on Highway 11, 27 km east of the junction with Highway 93, and 67 km west of the village of Nordegg.

0.0   Upper Bankhead Picnic Area, Cascade Valley trailhead. This section is a pleasant walk through the woods, which passes an outfitter's cabin and corrals.

1.2   The trail joins the east end of the Cascade Fire Road. The old road is wide and gravelled and heavily used by horses.

6.4   Cascade River bridge and Cascade Bridge Campground (Cr6). The road remains flat and easy walking.

13.3   Stony Creek Warden Cabin trail leads off to the left (northwest). The trail to the cabin rejoins the main trail a little later on. The cabin is at a beautiful spot, with a new cabin, as well as the old one, corrals, and an outbuilding.

14.2   The trail from the Stony Creek Warden Cabin rejoins on the left (southwest). Good views here.

14.7   Elk Pass trail branches to the left (west); continue straight ahead (north). This is the end of the bicycle and Nordic ski trail. Just beyond the trail junction are a bridge across Stony Creek and the Stony Creek Campground (Cr15). The trail to Dormer Pass goes to the right (east) just beyond the campground. Continue straight ahead. From here the road climbs steadily on the right (east) side of a narrow valley with mountains rising sharply on both sides. It offers occasional views of the Cascade River below.

17.7   Old elk enclosures. These structures are some distance from the trail on the right but are visible from the trail.

23.1   The heavily used horse trail branches left (northwest) to Flints Park. Most horses go to the left. Hikers heading north to the Red Deer River continue ahead on a more overgrown track that feels more like a trail.

25.5   Easy ford of a side stream. Beyond the stream crossing is a sign marking the site of Cuthead College, the old warden training school.

27.4   Cross Cuthead Creek on a culvert. The creek is now on the left (west).

28.8   Ford the creek to the right side (east).

30.1   Cross a small creek. Big Horn Lake is to the right (east); Cuthead Lake to the left (west). Trails to these lakes are very faint and not at all obvious. Continue straight ahead.

The old Cascade Fire Road, looking south toward the site of Windy Warden Cabin.

33.0   Wigmore Summit. The summit is a broad, flat valley with nothing marking the actual summit. Your first indication of having passed it is Wigmore Lake, just beyond the summit. From the lake, the road remains high above the narrow valley on the east side.

36.1   Ford Wigmore Creek. Cross the creek again in 0.7 km, this time on the rocks. The valley is very narrow and drops steeply to the Panther River.

39.1   Windy Warden Cabin is on the right. The Panther River trail goes right (east) from here. Continue following the old Cascade Fire Road straight ahead (north).

39.4   Panther River crossing (major ford). Panther Falls is 400 m to the right. Trail continues north, very high above the narrow Snow Creek valley.

42.8   An old wooden sign points to "Harrison Lake, on the left, 3 miles [4.8 km]."

46.8   At an old post that looks like a former signpost, a trail goes to the right (east) to Grouse Lake (1.2 km). Continue straight ahead.

49.3   Snow Creek Summit. This is a broad, flat summit, with very few trees, though the views are decent.

49.5   A post marks Snowflake Lake to the left (west) (2.0 km); continue straight ahead. There is a steady descent from Snow Creek Summit, with excellent views over a treed valley. Part of the hike is through an old burn area.

57.5   Junction. Scotch Camp Warden Station is on the left (west). Continue straight ahead.

58.2   Red Deer River bridge. There is an old outfitter's camp before the bridge and a good campsite at the junction with the river.

58.4   After the bridge, the Cascade Fire Road continues to the right (east). Take the Red Deer River trail on the left (west).

59.8   Divide Creek ford. I was able to cross on an old log. There is an old outfitter's camp here at the junction of Divide Creek and the Red Deer River.

60.0   Painted white sign in the trees reading "Clearwater River, 22 miles [35.4 km]." The Upper Red Deer River trail continues ahead (west); follow the Divide Creek/Peters Creek trail to the right (north). The trail continues steadily uphill through a mature forest. It is wide and heavily used by horses.

66.6   Trail begins sharp descent through the forest from a treeless ridge. There are good views from the ridge. Near the bottom, a gate crosses the trail.

68.0   Divide Creek. The creek can be crossed on the rocks

68.4   Divide Warden Cabin. There is a horse camp nearby. Continue over a ridge, then make your way uphill (north) through open country with good views to the top of the pass.

71.6   Divide Summit. From the summit, the trail is on the west side of the creek. It is not always easy to follow.

73.0   Cross Peters Creek to the east side; pick up the trail. The trail passes through heavy trees with sounds of the creek down below before dropping to the creek bank along a scree slope. It remains on the east side.

78.8   Cross Peters Creek to the west bank.

78.9   Cross Peters Creek to the east bank.

79.2   Cross Peters Creek again to the west bank. The trail climbs a rock slope, then follows along the creek.

80.8   There is a sign in a tree pointing to a hiker's trail on the left (west). The trail climbs steeply away from the creek.

82.4   Start a steep descent into the Clearwater Valley on a well-trodden trail through heavy forest. There are no views, but you will find an old fence just before the meadows.

84.0 Clearwater Valley meadows. There is an old fire warning sign in a tree. The sign dates from the early 1920s.

84.9 Old outfitter's camp at the far end of the meadow.

85.3 Clearwater River ford to north bank. By choosing a section of the river that is heavily braided, you can usually find a ford that is calf-deep or lower.

85.7 After crossing the river, head west along a well-used horse trail that soon joins the much wider Clearwater River trail. There is a large outfitter's camp here with a picnic table, firewood, and corral. You soon come to a beautiful wide-open area.

88.1 Park boundary. The wide horse trail reverts to a single-track trail.

89.1 Indianhead Lodge Warden Cabin. There are gates just before the old lodge.

89.2 Indianhead Creek ford.

89.9 The Indianhead Creek trail branches to the right (northwest). Follow this well-used horse trail northwest and gently uphill. The Clearwater River trail continues ahead (southwest).

93.3 Trail turns due north and begins a steep climb with switchbacks. The terrain becomes more open as you climb, with good views in both directions. The trail crosses an open valley and climbs to the top of a high ridge.

95.9 Ridge Summit. Begin a steep switchback descent then follow a wide-open valley above Indianhead Creek.

100.6 Cross to east side of Indianhead Creek and begin a steady uphill.

102.6 Whiterabbit Pass. The National Park boundary is at the top of the pass. As you start downhill to the Ram River, the open slopes on the right (east) have very visible animal trails. The trail passes through a treed area, and then the wide valley of the Ram River becomes visible on the right (east).

106.3   Large outfitter's camp, just before the Ram River. There are tracks everywhere made by off-highway vehicles (quads). Follow the quad road to an easy ford of the Ram River. From the river, follow a quad road northward. The horse trail is visible in places and parallels the quad road along this section. Ford the creek just below the cabin. This area is a good example of the total devastation that can be caused by off-road vehicles.

108.6   Headwaters Cabin. From the cabin, the trail first heads west, then circles around to the east behind the cabin before heading north along a high ridge, gradually veering to the northwest. Do not follow the Ram River valley to the northeast. It is important to stay on the horse trail, resisting the temptation to take a quad trail. The trail goes through a gully, then climbs steeply up a ridge. Partway up the ridge is an old steel sign, with no visible lettering. There are good views of the Ram River valley on the right. The well-beaten horse trail levels out on a wide plateau.

110.6   At the end of a long meadow, you get a good view of the beautiful Whiterabbit Creek valley. The trail starts downhill. It remains a good horse trail, often intersected by quad trails. Stay on the horse trail! The trail crosses a broad, open meadow and crosses several side streams.

114.4   Cross Whiterabbit Creek to the east side.

116.2   Ford Whiterabbit Creek to the west side. There is an old outfitter's camp on the west side, with corrals and firewood. After the camp, the valley opens up again with good views to the west. Shortly after the camp, ford the creek to the east side.

117.1   Outfitter's camp. The trail soon comes to gravel flats. Hikers should stay close to the creek on the east side.

120.7   Old camp spot.

122.5   Blow-down area. This area has recently been cleared of fallen trees, as has the whole trail from the Ram River north. The trail continues in the forest parallel to the creek.

128.2   Viewpoint, high above the Whiterabbit Creek valley.

130.8   A trail goes off to the right (east); continue straight ahead.

131.1   Camp spot, North Saskatchewan River valley floor. There are three more campsites in the next 3 km.

134.4   Easy ford to the west side of Whiterabbit Creek. There is another campsite here. The trail proceeds through a young mixed forest. After fording the creek, keep left (generally west) at each trail junction.

135.1   The trail runs into an old road. Turn left and follow in a southerly direction.

136.5   Road turns sharply southwest and drops down into a valley. The road splits; take the left branch (heading west), which turns into a horse trail, then joins a major gravel road. Continue left on the road.

138.2   Sign post says Whiterabbit Trail. The Siffleur Falls trail is just ahead, as well as a bridge over the Siffleur River. You soon come to a boardwalk leading to the North Saskatchewan River.

139.4   North Saskatchewan River suspension bridge. The parking area is just ahead on the wide tourist trail.

NOTES

INTRODUCTION

1. Chief John Snow, *These Mountains Are Our Sacred Places: The Story of the Stoney People* (Toronto: Samuel Stevens, 1977), 13.

2. E.J. Hart, *Diamond Hitch: The Early Outfitters and Guides of Banff and Jasper* (Banff: Summerthought, 1979), 35.

3. R.J. Burns with M. Schintz, *Guardians of the Wild: A History of the Warden Service of Canada's National Parks* (Calgary: University of Calgary Press, 2000), 7.

4. Ibid., 31.

5. Ibid., 33.

6. Hart, 139.

7. A.P. Coleman, *The Canadian Rockies: New and Old Trails* (Calgary: Aquila Books, 1999), 234.

8. The Reverend George M. Grant, *Ocean to Ocean: Sandford Fleming's Expedition through Canada in 1872* (Rutland, Vt.: Charles E. Tuttle, 1967), 236.

ROUTE I

1. David Thompson, *Columbia Journals: David Thompson*, edited by Barbara Belyea (Montreal: McGill-Queen's University Press, 1994), 7–8.

2. Jon Whyte, *Indians in the Rockies* (Canmore: Altitude, 1985), 24.

3. Barbara Huck and Doug Whiteway, *In Search of Ancient Alberta* (Winnipeg: Heartland, 1998), 105.

4. Whyte, 24.

5. Barry Gough, *First Across the Continent: Sir Alexander Mackenzie* (Toronto: McClelland & Stewart, 1997), 105–62.

6. A thorough description of Henday's route can be found in Anthony Henday, *A Year Inland: The Journal of a Hudson's Bay Company Winterer*, edition and commentary by Barbara Belyea (Waterloo, Ont.: Wilfred Laurier University Press, 2000), 325–42.

7. Jack Nisbet, *Sources of the River* (Seattle: Sasquatch Books, 1994), 19.

8. J.G. MacGregor, *Peter Fidler* (Calgary: Fifth House, 1998), 66.

9. Quoted in Joyce and Peter McCart, *On the Road with David Thompson* (Calgary: Fifth House, 2000), 12–13.

10. Nisbet, 250.

11. Thompson, 3.

12. Ibid., 3, 4.

13. Ann Dixon, *Silent Partners: Wives of National Park Wardens* (Pincher Creek, Alta.: Dixon and Dixon, 1985), 5.

14. Belyea, 6.

15. Brian Patton and Bart Robinson, *The Canadian Rockies Trail Guide*, 7th ed. (Banff: Summerthought, 2000), 43.

16. For a recent biography of Mary Schäffer Warren, see Janice Sanford Beck, *No Ordinary Woman: The Story of Mary Schäffer Warren*, (Calgary: Rocky Mountain Books, 2001).

17. Mary Schäffer Warren, "Ptarmigan Valley Twenty Years Ago," *Trail Riders of the Canadian Rockies Bulletin* 10 (July 16, 1926): 1.

18. For a brief biographical sketch of Bill Peyto, see Emerson Sanford and Janice Sanford Beck, *Life of the Trail 2: Historic Hikes in Northern Yoho National Park* (Calgary:Rocky Mountain Books, 2008), 46–48.

19. For a brief biographical sketch of Tom Wilson, famous outfitter and pioneer in the Bow Valley, *Life of the Trail 2*, 42-44.

20. Sanford Beck, 27–30.

21. The first Swiss guides were brought to the Canadian West in 1899. See Andrew J. Kauffman and William L. Putnam, *The Guiding Spirit*, (Revelstoke, BC: Footprint Publishing, 1986), 20.

22. J.W.A. Hickson, "Ascent of Mount Douglas (11,200 feet)," *Canadian Alpine Journal* 3 (1911): 41–42.

23. Ibid., 42–43.

24. J.F. Brett, "Dr. J.W.A. Hickson," *Canadian Alpine Journal* 40 (1957): 66.

25. James F. Porter, "The Ptarmigan Lake Region," *Canadian Alpine Journal* 4 (1912): 110–116.

26. Ibid., 115.

27. Don Beers, *The World of Lake Louise: A Guide for Hikers* (Calgary: Highline, 1991), 200.

28. "Report of the Ptarmigan Lake Camp," *Canadian Alpine Journal* 7 (1916): 124.

29. Ibid., 125.

30. Walter Wilcox, "The Valley of the Hidden Lakes," *Canadian Alpine Journal* 13 (1923): 179.

31. Geological and Natural History Survey of Canada, *Annual Report 1* (1885) (Montreal: Dawson Brothers, 1886), 3.

32. E.O. Wheeler, "Morrison P. Bridgland," *Canadian Alpine Journal* 31 (1948): 222.

33. C.B. Sissons, "Morrison P. Bridgland," *Canadian Alpine Journal* 31 (1948): 218.

34. For a more complete discussion of Walcott and a brief biographical sketch, see *Life of the Trail 2*, 118-129.

35. For a brief biological sketch of Mary Vaux Walcott, see *Life of the Trail 2*, 127-129.

36. Ellis L. Yochelson, *Smithsonian Institution Secretary: Charles Doolittle Walcott* (Kent, Ohio: Kent State University Press, 2001), 193.

37. For details of Walcott's travels in this area, see *Life of the Trail 2*, 118-129.

38. Yochelson, 319-320.

39. For a description of this trip see *Life of the Trail 2*, 160-163..

40. Yochelson, 366.

41. Ibid., 386.

42. Ibid., 409.

43. Ibid., 410.

44. Ibid.

45. Ibid., 455–62.

46. For a history of outfitting in the Rockies, see E.J. Hart, *Diamond Hitch: The Early Outfitters and Guides of Banff and Jasper*, (Banff: Summerthought, 1979).

47. Cyndi Smith, *Off the Beaten Track: Women Adventurers and Mountaineers in Western Canada* (Lake Louise: Coyote Books, 1989) 108–10.

48. Caroline Hinman fonds, Whyte Museum of the Canadian Rockies, M236 V282/PD3.

49. Lillian Gest fonds, Whyte Museum of the Canadian Rockies, M67/41, 75. These structures were built in 1930, 1931, and 1939, respectively. See Rodney Touche, *Brown Cows, Sacred Cows: A True Story of Lake Louise* (Hanna, Alta.: Gorman Publishers, 1990), 15, 19, and 62.

50. Smith, 121–22, 206.

51. Lisa Christensen has written three books on art of the Canadian Rockies. More are in progress.

52. E.J. Hart, *Jimmy Simpson: Legend of the Rockies* (Canmore: Altitude, 1991), 66.

53. Jon Whyte and E.J. Hart, *Painter of the Western Wilderness* (Calgary: the Glenbow-Alberta Institute in association with Douglas & McIntyre, 1985), 123.

54. Quoted in Lisa Christensen, *A Hiker's Guide to Art of the Canadian Rockies* (Calgary: Glenbow Museum, 1996), 47.

55. Ibid.

56. McCart, 9–27.

ROUTE II

1. Irene M. Spry, *The Palliser Expedition: The Dramatic Story of Western Canadian Exploration, 1857-1860*, 2nd ed. (Saskatoon: Fifth House, 1995), 243–51.

2. Ibid., 254.

3. Ibid., 169.

4. James Carnegie, Earl of Southesk, *Saskatchewan and the Rocky Mountains* (Rutland, Vt.: Charles E. Tuttle, 1969), 245.

5. Peter Erasmus, *Buffalo Days and Nights* (Calgary: Fifth House, 1999), 75.

6. Ralph Edwards, *The Trail to the Charmed Land* (Victoria: H.R. Larson, 1950), 40. A cayuse is a pony (small horse) bred and raised by Aboriginal peoples.

7. Ibid., 44.

8. H.E.M. Stutfield and J. Norman Collie, *Climbs and Exploration in the Canadian Rockies* (Calgary: Aquila Books, 1998), 71–72.

9. Ibid., 73.

10. Ibid., 74–75.

11. Ibid., 76.

12. Ibid., 81.

13. Ibid., 80–81.

14. Anne (McMullen) Belliveau, *Small Moments in Time: The Story of Alberta's Big West Country* (Calgary: Detselig, 1999), 20.

15. Ibid., 35.

16. Don Beers, *The World of Lake Louise: A Guide for Hikers* (Calgary: Highline, 1991), 102.

17. Tom Wilson, "Memories of Golden Days," *Canadian Alpine Journal* 14 (1924): 123–25.

18. A.O. Wheeler and Tom Wilson, "Christmas Dinner," *Tales from the Canadian Rockies*, ed. Brian Patton (Edmonton: Hurtig, 1984), 187.

19. E.J. Hart, *Jimmy Simpson: Legend of the Rockies* (Canmore: Altitude, 1991), 61–62.

20. Ibid., 62.

21. Jane Ross and Daniel Kyba, *The David Thompson Highway: A Hiking Guide* (Calgary: Rocky Mountain Books, 1995), 16.

22. Morley is a small village 40 kilometres east of Canmore in the Bow Valley's Stoney Reserve.

23. W. John Koch, *Martin Nordegg: The Uncommon Immigrant* (Edmonton: Brightest Pebble, 1997), 91.

24. Martin Nordegg, *To the Town that Bears Your Name: A Young Woman's Journey to Nordegg in 1912* (Edmonton: Brightest Pebble, 1995), 78–82.

25. Ibid., 81.

26. Ibid., 99.

27. Janice Sanford Beck, *No Ordinary Woman: The Story of Mary Schäffer Warren* (Calgary: Rocky Mountain Books, 2001), 32.

28. Cyndi Smith, *Off the Beaten Track: Women Adventurers and Mountaineers in Western Canada* (Lake Louise: Coyote Books, 1989), 140.

29. Ibid., 57.

30. A.P. Coleman, *The Canadian Rockies: New and Old Trails* (Calgary: Aquila Books, 1999), 240.

31. Ibid., 243.

32. Ibid., 246.

33. Ibid.

34. For more information about the Walcotts and their travels, see Emerson Sanford and Janice Sanford Beck, *Life of the Trail 2: Historic Hikes in Northern Yoho National Park* (Calgary: Rocky Mountain Books, 2008), 118–129..

35. Ellis L. Yochelson, *Smithsonian Institution Secretary: Charles Doolittle Walcott* (Kent, Ohio: Kent State University Press, 2001), 293.

36. For details about this trip, see *Life of the Trail 2*, 160–163..

37. Lillian Gest fonds, Whyte Museum of the Canadian Rockies, M67:41, 32–33.

38. Val A. Fynn, "The Story of a Failure," *Canadian Alpine Journal* 11 (1920): 186.

39. Caroline Hinman fonds, Whyte Museum of the Canadian Rockies, M236 V282/PD6, 32–48.

40. Lillian Gest fonds, 95, 136.

ROUTE III

1. The name Forty Mile Creek is an old railway name, the creek being forty miles from the old railway siding at Morley.

2. Quoted in Graeme Pole, *Classic Hikes in the Canadian Rockies* (Canmore: Altitude, 1994), 47.

3. E.J. Hart, *The Brewster Story: From Pack Train to Tour Bus* (Banff: Brewster Transport, 1981), 4–5.

4. Bow Valley Naturalists, *Vermilion Lakes, Banff National Park: An Introductory Study* (Banff: Bow Valley Naturalists, 1978), 14.

5. F.O. "Pat" Brewster, *Weathered Wood: Anecdotes and History of the Banff-Sunshine Area* (Banff: Crag and Canyon, 1977), 14.

6. Dawson (see Route 1 on page 47) travelled along the Red Deer River, then on down the Little Pipestone Creek in 1884 and normally made maps of his travels. Little is known about the map Wilcox refers to.

7. Walter D. Wilcox, *Camping in the Canadian Rockies* (New York: G.P. Putnam's Sons, 1896), 211–14.

8. E.J. Hart, *Ain't It Hell: Bill Peyto's "Mountain Journal"* (Banff: EJH Literary Enterprises, 1995), 40.

9. E.J. Hart, *Jimmy Simpson: Legend of the Rockies* (Canmore: Altitude, 1991), 23.

10. Hart, 1995, 140.

11. Cyndi Smith, *Off the Beaten Track: Women Adventurers and Mountaineers in Western Canada* (Lake Louise: Coyote Books, 1989), 87.

12. R.J. Burns with M. Schintz, *Guardians of the Wild: A History of the Warden Service of Canada's National Parks* (Calgary: University of Calgary Press, 2000), 33.

13. Hart, 1991, 115.

14. This group, inaugurated under the auspices of the CPR, organized several trail rides through the Rockies each summer. Participants were recruited through advertising, and did not normally know one another prior to the excursion. Though no longer affiliated with the railway, the Trail Riders organization still exists today.

15. "General Rides and Central Pow-Wow," *Trail Riders of the Canadian Rockies Bulletin* 7 (1926), 1.

16. Ellis L. Yochelson, *Smithsonian Institution Secretary: Charles Doolittle Walcott* (Kent, Ohio: Kent State University Press, 2001), 238, 320.

17. Don Beers, *Banff-Assiniboine: A Beautiful World* (Calgary: Highline, 1993), 130.

18. From Earle Birney, "Bushed," in *One Muddy Hand: Selected Poems of Earle Birney* (Madeira Park, B.C.: Harbour Publishing, 2006), 67. Reprinted with permission.

ROUTE IV

1. For details on this part of the trip, see Emerson Sanford and Janice Sanford Beck, *Life of the Trail 2: Historic Hikes in Northern Yoho National Park* (Calgary: Rocky Mountain Books, 2008), 58–60.

2. Lillian Gest, *History of Lake O'Hara in the Canadian Rockies at Hector, British Columbia*, 4th ed. (s.l.: s.n., 1989), 10.

3. Ibid.

4. R.E. Campbell, "Tom Wilson of Banff," *Canadian Cattlemen* 21:2 (February 1958): 12, 28–30, 38–39; and 21:3 (March 1958): 28.

5. A.P. Coleman, *The Canadian Rockies: New & Old Trails* (Calgary: Aquila Books, 1999), 122.

6. Ibid.

7. J. Munroe Thorington, *The Glittering Mountains of Canada* (Philadelphia: John W. Lea, 1925), 107. Jean L. Johnson reported that Lucius Quincy Coleman and his aunt, Miss A.M. Adams, who were partners, arrived in the Morleyville settlement in the early 1880s. On October 22, 1896, at the age of forty-three years, Lucius married Ella, a girl from Ontario. Miss Adams died in May 1912 at the age of eighty-three. Lucius sold the ranch in 1916.

8. Coleman, 129.

9. Ibid., 132.

10. Ibid., 133.

11. Ibid., 169.

12. Ernie Lakusta, *Canmore and Kananaskis History Explorer* (Canmore: Altitude, 2002), 152. Sibbald Flats in Kananaskis Country was probably named after Frank, who homesteaded in the Jumpingpound Creek area in 1890 – near the creek and meadow that now may bear his name.

13. Coleman, 216.

14. Ibid., 176.

15. Ibid., 177.

16. Ibid., 213–14.

17. Ibid., 213.

18. Ibid., 212.

19. Ibid., 219.

20. Ibid., 220.

21. Ibid., 234.

22. Dr. George M. Dawson, *Preliminary Report on the Physical and Geological Features of That Portion of the Rocky Mountains between Latitudes 49 degrees and 51 degrees 30 minutes* (Ottawa: Canadian Institute for Historical Microreproductions, 1985), 143.

23. R.J. Burns with M. Schintz, *Guardians of the Wild: A History of the Warden Service of Canada's National Parks* (Calgary: University of Calgary Press, 2000), 32.

IMAGE CREDITS

Page 26 Artist's rendition of what David Thompson may have looked like while surveying. (Compliments of Algonquin Park Visitor Centre)

Page 33 Mary Schäffer, one of the first non-Aboriginal people to camp in the Ptarmigan Valley and the first woman to explore extensively in the Rocky Mountains. (Whyte Museum of the Canadian Rockies, V527/NG-10)

Page 34 A.O. Wheeler surveyed extensively in the mountains but was best known as the founding president of the Alpine Club of Canada. (Whyte Museum of the Canadian Rockies, NA66-299)

Page 35 Walter Wilcox (r) with his Yale University climbing friends (l–r) Yandell Henderson, L.F. Frissel, and H.G. Warrington.(Whyte Museum of the Canadian Rockies, NA66-2251)

Page 38 Canadian mountaineer J.W.A. Hickson, the first to climb in the Ptarmigan Valley area, with his favourite Swiss guide, Edward Feuz Jr. (Whyte Museum of the Canadian Rockies, V14/AC-55P/33(16))

Page 39 Jimmy Simpson, one of the leading guides and outfitters in the Canadian Rockies. (Whyte Museum of the Canadian Rockies, NA66-265)

Page 42 Mountaineer J.F. Porter extensively explored the Ptarmigan and Skoki valley areas. (Whyte Museum of the Canadian Rockies, V14/AC229-P/1)

Page 43 James Harkin, first Commissioner of the National Parks Branch, was instrumental in the establishment of the Warden Service and a strong advocate for conservation. (National Archives of Canada, PA-12137)

Page 46 Dr. George Mercer Dawson of the Geological Survey of Canada had completed a geological survey of the eastern Rockies by 1884. (National Archives of Canada, PA-26689)

Page 49 M.P. Bridgland, third from the left, with fellow guides (l–r): Edward Feuz, H.G. Wheeler, and Gottfried Feuz at the 1906 ACC camp in the Yoho Valley. (Whyte Museum of the Canadian Rockies, CAJ Vol. I, 1907, p.168)

Page 50 Dr. Charles Doolittle Walcott spent eighteen years studying geology and collecting fossils in the Canadian Rockies. (Whyte Museum of the Canadian Rockies, V263/NA-71-563)

Page 55 Caroline Hinman, leader of Off the Beaten Track alpine adventures for American girls. (Whyte Museum of the Canadian Rockies, V225/PD-7 (49))

Page 56 Jim Boyce dedicated sixteen summers to guiding Caroline Hinman's Off the Beaten Track tours. (Whyte Museum of the Canadian Rockies, NA66-1113)

Page 59 Carl Rungius, artist, hunter, and mountain explorer. (Whyte Museum of the Canadian Rockies, NA66-1182)

Page 76 Rocky Mountain explorer James Hector (r) with Captain John Palliser, the first men to enter the mountains with the sole objective of exploring. Hector explored extensively in the area south of Athabasca Pass and north of Banff. (Glenbow Museum and Archives, NA-588-1)

Page 78 James Carnegie, Earl of Southesk, determined to find "sport" among the larger animals of the Rocky Mountains. (Glenbow Museum and Archives, NA-1355-1)

Page 80 Peter Erasmus, guide and interpreter, also trapped, hunted, traded, and taught. He was already a legend within his own lifetime. (Glenbow Museum and Archives, NA-3148-1)

Page 83 Ralph Edwards, mountain guide and packer, got his start working for Tom Wilson. (Whyte Museum of the Canadian Rockies, NA66-482)

Page 86 Bill Peyto, one of Banff's most famous guides, was also a trapper, prospector, miner, explorer, and park warden. (Whyte Museum of the Canadian Rockies, NA66-467)

Page 86 Dr. J. Norman Collie (l) and H.E.M. Stutfield "assisting the choppers" in clearing the trail. Paying customers did not help the hired men! (Whyte Museum of the Canadian Rockies, NA66-470)

Page 90 Tom Wilson (l) with Morley Beaver, a member of the Stoney tribe with whom Wilson traded during his winters on the Kootenay Plains. (Whyte Museum of the Canadian Rockies, V701/LC-17)

Page 91 Herd of horses on the Pipestone Pass trail en route to their winter pasture at the Wilson ranch on the Kootenay Plains. (Whyte Museum of the Canadian Rockies, detail from V701/LC-146)

Page 93 Tom Wilson on snowshoes. Wilson nearly lost his life snowshoeing over Pipestone Pass in a 1908 snowstorm. (Whyte Museum of the Canadian Rockies, V701/LC-34)

Page 94 Tom Lusk, a heavy-drinking, short-tempered fugitive from Texas, stayed sober long enough to prove an excellent head guide for Martin Nordegg's exploration trips over Pipestone Pass and east into the foothills. (Whyte Museum of the Canadian Rockies, NA66-474)

Page 96 Martin Nordegg, ready for his first trip over Pipestone Pass. (National Archives of Canada, C-035065)

Page 99 Pack train crossing Pipestone Pass. Nordegg would have been accompanied by a similar pack train on his first foray into the mountains. (Whyte Museum of the Canadian Rockies, V653/NA 80-468)

Page 100 Marcelle Nordegg, enjoying a few days of rest while waiting to begin her trip from Nordegg to Lake Louise over Pipestone Pass. (Photo courtesy of W. John Koch)

Page 105 (l–r) Mollie Adams, Mary Schäffer, and guides Billy Warren and Joe Barker in camp. Adams and Schäffer were the first non-Aboriginal women to travel and explore extensively in the Canadian Rocky Mountains. (Whyte Museum of the Canadian Rockies, V439/PS-1)

Page 106 Dr. A.P. Coleman, a highly respected climber and explorer in the Rocky Mountains. He and his party did not hire outfitters, preferring to do all of the work themselves. (Whyte Museum of the Canadian Rockies, V439/PS-20)

Page 108 Rev. George Kinney (r), a loner who joined the Coleman brothers on their quest to reach Mount Robson. Kinney was obsessed with climbing the mountain and later succeeded with guide Curly Phillips (l). (Whyte Museum of the Canadian Rockies, V263/NA-71-6016)

Page 112 Hunters (l–r) Caroline Hinman, Lillian Gest, and Louise Vincent, ready for adventure on one of their fall hunting trips. (Whyte Museum of the Canadian Rockies, V225/PD-5 (312))

Page 126 Stoneys William Twin and his twin brother Joshua played an important role in the early history of Banff and Lake Louise. (Whyte Museum of the Canadian Rockies, V701/LC-312)

Page 130 J.J. McArthur, an early surveyor and explorer in the mountains. McArthur Lake, Pass, and Creek in southern Yoho National Park are named after him. (National Archives of Canada, PA-42178)

Page 133 Stoney William Twin (l) and his twin brother Joshua (r), in traditional regalia. (Whyte Museum of the Canadian Rockies, detail from V701/LC-313)

Page 134 Walter Wilcox first visited the Canadian Rockies in 1893 and spent the next forty years exploring, climbing, and naming features. His *Camping in the Canadian Rockies* was the first book written about the area. (Whyte Museum of the Canadian Rockies, NA66-469)

Page 135 Bill Peyto, in front of one of his backcountry cabins, with gun, dog, and pack, ready for an outing. (Whyte Museum of the Canadian Rockies, NA66-262)

Page 141 Mary Jobe made her mark exploring the mountains north of Mount Robson. (Whyte Museum of the Canadian Rockies, V14/NA66-504)

Page 145 Pack train crossing the steep and rugged Badger Pass. The Walcotts' pack train would have looked similar to this one. (Whyte Museum of the Canadian Rockies, V263/NA-71-16)

Page 148 Leonard Leacock devoted his life to music but found time to hike the mountain trails and introduce young people to the joys of mountain hiking. (Whyte Museum of the Canadian Rockies, V408/NA-14 (113))

Page 164 A typical Caroline Hinman Off the Beaten Track trail group on an unidentified mountain pass. (Whyte Museum of the Canadian Rockies, NA66-1159)

Page 166 Lillian Gest, a friend who accompanied Caroline Hinman on many of her backcountry excursions, spent every summer from 1921 to 1984 in the Canadian Rockies. (Whyte Museum of the Canadian Rockies, V225/PA-134)

Page 169 Outfitter Tom Wilson travelled widely in the mountains. His nearly photographic memory made him an encyclopedia of knowledge for later travellers.(Whyte Museum of the Canadian Rockies, V701/LC34-117)

Page 171 Professor A.P. Coleman, who solved the "David Douglas Controversy." (Whyte Museum of the Canadian Rockies, V14 AC 00P-82)

Page 176 The Sampson Beaver family (l–r): Leah, Frances Louise, and Sampson. Sampson was reputed to be one of the best Stoney hunters of his time, and he knew the area north of the Red Deer River intimately. (Whyte Museum of the Canadian Rockies, V437/PS-7)

Back cover photo (Whyte Museum of the Canadian Rockies, V701/LC-313)

All other photographs: Emerson Sanford

BIBLIOGRAPHY

Barbeau, Marius. *Indian Days in the Canadian Rockies.* Toronto: Macmillan, 1923.

Beers, Don. *Banff-Assiniboine: A Beautiful World.* Calgary: Highline, 1993.

Beers, Don. *The World of Lake Louise: A Guide for Hikers.* Calgary: Highline, 1991.

Belliveau, Anne (McMullen). *Small Moments in Time: The Story of Alberta's Big West Country.* Calgary: Detselig Enterprises, 1999.

Birney, Earle. *One Muddy Hand: Selected Poems of Earle Birney,* edited by Sam Solecki. Madeira Park, B.C.: Harbour Publishing, 2006.

Birrell, Dave. *50 Roadside Panoramas in the Canadian Rockies.* Calgary, Rocky Mountain Books, 2000.

Bow Valley Naturalists. *Vermilion Lakes, Banff National Park; An Introductory Study.* Banff: Bow Valley Naturalists, 1978.

Brett, J.F. "Dr. J.W.A. Hickson." *Canadian Alpine Journal* 40 (1957): 66.

Brewster, F.O. "Pat." *Weathered Wood: Anecdotes and History of the Banff-Sunshine Area.* Banff: Crag and Canyon/Altitude, 1977.

Burns, R. J., with M. Schintz. *Guardians of the Wild: A History of the Warden Service of Canada's National Parks.* Calgary: University of Calgary Press, 2000.

Campbell, R.E. "Tom Wilson of Banff." *Canadian Cattlemen* 21:2 (February 1958): 12, 28–30, 38–39.

Campbell, R.E. "Tom Wilson of Banff (cont.)." *Canadian Cattlemen* 21:3 (March 1958): 28.

Canadian Alpine Journal. Canmore: Alpine Club of Canada, 1907–present.

Caroline Hinman fonds. Whyte Museum of the Canadian Rockies. Banff, Alta. M236 V282/PD3.

Christensen, Lisa. *A Hiker's Guide to Art of the Canadian Rockies.* Calgary: Glenbow Museum, 1996.

Christensen, Lisa. *A Hiker's Guide to the Rocky Mountain Art of Lawren Harris.* Calgary: Fifth House, 2000.

Christensen, Lisa. *The Lake O'Hara Art of J.E.H. MacDonald.* Calgary: Fifth House, 2003.

Coleman, A.P. *The Canadian Rockies: New & Old Trails.* Toronto: Henry Frowde, 1911; reprinted Calgary: Aquila Books, 1999.

Dawson, Dr. George M. *Preliminary Report on the Physical and Geological Features of that Portion of the Rocky Mountains between Latitudes 49 degrees and 51 degrees 30 minutes.* Originally published Montreal: Dawson Brothers, 1886; reprinted Ottawa: Canadian Institute for Historical Microreproductions, 1985.

Dixon, Ann. *Silent Partners: Wives of National Park Wardens.* Pincher Creek: Dixon and Dixon, 1985.

Edwards, Ralph. *The Trail to the Charmed Land.* Victoria: H.R. Larson, 1950.

Erasmus, Peter. *Buffalo Days and Nights.* Calgary: Fifth House, 1999.

Fynn, Val A. "The Story of a Failure." *Canadian Alpine Journal* 11 (1920): 186.

"General Rides and Central Pow-Wow." *Trail Riders of the Canadian Rockies Bulletin* 7 (1923): 1.

Gest, Lillian. *History of Lake O'Hara in the Canadian Rockies at Hector, British Columbia,* 4th ed. S.l.: s.n., 1989.

Geological and Natural History Survey of Canada. *Annual Report, Volume I* (1885). Montreal: Dawson Brothers, 1886.

Gough, Barry. *First Across the Continent: Sir Alexander Mackenzie.* Toronto: McClelland & Stewart, 1997.

Grant, Reverend George M. *Ocean to Ocean: Sandford Fleming's Expedition through Canada in 1872.* Rutland, Vt.: Charles E. Tuttle, 1967.

Haig, Bruce. *Following Historic Trails: James Hector Explorer.* Calgary: Detselig, 1983.

Hart, E.J. *Ain't it Hell: Bill Peyto's "Mountain Journal."* Banff: EJH Literary Enterprises, 1995.

Hart, E.J. *Diamond Hitch: The Early Outfitters and Guides of Banff and Jasper.* Banff: Summerthought, 1979.

Hart, E.J. *Jimmy Simpson: Legend of the Rockies.* Canmore: Altitude, 1991.

Hart, E.J. *The Brewster Story: From Pack Train to Tour Bus.* Banff: Brewster Transport, 1981.

Henday, Anthony. *A Year Inland: The Journal of a Hudson's Bay Company Winterer,* edition and commentary by Barbara Belyea. Waterloo, Ont.: Wilfred Laurier University Press, 2000.

Hickson, J.W.A. "Ascent of Mount Douglas (11,200 feet)." *Canadian Alpine Journal* 3 (1911): 41–42.

Huck, Barbara, and Doug Whiteway. *In Search of Ancient Alberta*. Winnipeg: Heartland, 1998.

Kauffman, A.J., and W.L. Putnam. *The Guiding Spirit*. Revelstoke: Footprint, 1986.

Koch, W. John. *Martin Nordegg: The Uncommon Immigrant*. Edmonton: Brightest Pebble, 1997.

Lakusta, Ernie. *Canmore and Kananaskis History Explorer*. Canmore: Altitude, 2002.

Lillian Gest fonds. Whyte Museum of the Canadian Rockies. Banff, Alta. M67/41.

MacGregor, James G. *Peter Fidler: Canada's Forgotten Explorer, 1769-1822*. Calgary: Fifth House, 1998.

MacLaren, I.S. *Mapper of Mountains: M.P. Bridgland in the Canadian Rockies 1902-1930*. Edmonton: University of Alberta Press, 2005.

Manry, Kathryn. *Skoki Beyond the Passes*. Calgary: Rocky Mountain Books, 2001.

McCart, Joyce, and Peter. *On the Road with David Thompson*. Calgary: Fifth House, 2000.

Newman, Peter C. *Caesars of the Wilderness*. Markham: Viking, 1987.

Nisbet, Jack. *Sources of the River*. Seattle: Sasquatch Books, 1994.

Nordegg, Martin. *To the Town that Bears Your Name: A Young Woman's Journey to Nordegg in 1912*. Edmonton: Brightest Pebble, 1995.

Patton, Brian, ed. *Tales from the Canadian Rockies*. Edmonton: Hurtig, 1984.

Patton, Brian, and Bart Robinson. *The Canadian Rockies Trail Guide*, 7th ed. Banff: Summerthought, 2000.

Pole, Graeme. *Classic Hikes in the Canadian Rockies*. Canmore: Altitude, 1994.

Porter, James F. "The Ptarmigan Lake Region." *Canadian Alpine Journal* 4 (1912): 110–16.

Potter, Mike. *Hiking Lake Louise*. Banff: Luminous Publications, 1990.

Potter, Mike. *Backcountry Banff*. Banff: Luminous Publications, 1992.

"Report of the Ptarmigan Lake Camp." *Canadian Alpine Journal* 7 (1916): 124–27.

Ross, Jane, and Daniel Kyba. *The David Thompson Highway: A Hiking Guide*. Calgary: Rocky Mountain Books, 1995.

Sandford, R.W. *The Canadian Alps*. Banff: Altitude, 1990.

Sanford Beck, Janice. *No Ordinary Woman: The Story of Mary Schäffer Warren*. Calgary: Rocky Mountain Books, 2001.

Scott, Chic. *Pushing the Limits*. Calgary: Rocky Mountain Books, 2000.

Sissons, C.B. "Morrison P. Bridgland." *Canadian Alpine Journal* 3 (1948): 218–20.

Smith, Cyndi. *Off the Beaten Track: Women Adventurers and Mountaineers in Western Canada*. Lake Louise: Coyote Books, 1989.

Snow, Chief John. *These Mountains Are Our Sacred Places: The Story of the Stoney People*. Toronto: Samuel Stevens, 1977.

Southesk, James Carnegie, Earl of. *Saskatchewan and the Rocky Mountains*. Rutland, Vt.: Charles E. Tuttle, 1969. Originally published Edinburgh, Edmonston & Douglas, 1875.

Spry, Irene M. *The Palliser Expedition: The Dramatic Story of Western Canadian Exploration, 1857-1860*. 2nd ed. Saskatoon: Fifth House, 1995. Originally published Toronto: Macmillan, 1963.

Stutfield, H.E.M., and J. Norman Collie. *Climbs and Exploration in the Canadian Rockies*. New York: Longmans, Green & Co., 1903; reprinted Calgary: Aquila Books, 1998.

Thompson, David. *Columbia Journals: David Thompson* edited by Barbara Belyea. Montreal: McGill-Queen's University Press, 1994.

Thorington, J. Monroe. *The Glittering Mountains of Canada*. Philadelphia: John W. Lea, 1925.

Touche, Rodney. *Brown Cows, Sacred Cows: A True Story of Lake Louise*. Hanna, Alta.: Gorman, 1990.

Warren, Mary Shaeffer. "Ptarmigan Valley Twenty Years Ago." *Trail Riders of the Canadian Rockies Bulletin* 10 (July 16, 1926): 1–3.

Wheeler, E.O. "Morrison P. Bridgland." *Canadian Alpine Journal* 31 (1948): 220–22.

Whyte, Jon. *Indians in the Rockies*. Canmore: Altitude, 1985.

Whyte, Jon, and E.J. Hart. *Painter of the Western Wilderness*. Calgary: The Glenbow-Alberta Institute in association with Douglas & McIntyre, 1985.

Wilcox, Walter D. *Camping in the Canadian Rockies*. New York: G.P. Putnam's Sons, 1896.

Wilcox, Walter D. "The Valley of the Hidden Lakes." *Canadian Alpine Journal* 13 (1923): 179.

Wilson, Tom. "Memories of Golden Days." Canadian Alpine Journal 14 (1924): 123–25.

Yochelson, Ellis L. *Smithsonian Institution Secretary: Charles Doolittle Walcott*. Kent, Ohio: Kent State University Press, 2001.

Index

About the Authors

Emerson Sanford, originally from Nova Scotia, first visited the mountains of western Canada in the summer of 1961. Eleven years later, he moved to Alberta, and has been hiking ever since. After beginning to backpack seriously with his teenaged daughters in 1990, he began to wonder who cut the trails and how their routing had been determined. Since then, not only has he delved through printed material about the trails, he has also solo hiked every historic route and most long trails between Mount Robson and the Kananaskis Lakes – over 3000 km over five years! Emerson now lives in Canmore with his wife, Cheryl.

Janice Sanford Beck is the author of the best-selling *No Ordinary Woman: the Story of Mary Schäffer Warren* (Rocky Mountain Books, 2001). She has also written the introduction to the latest edition of Mary T.S. Schäffer's *Old Indian Trails of the Canadian Rockies* (Rocky Mountain Books, 2007) and, with Cheryl Sanford, researched the Mary Schäffer Warren portion of the Glenbow Museum's new permanent exhibit, "Mavericks." Janice is presently masquerading as a flatlander, making her home in Saskatoon with her partner, Shawn, and their two children.

FURTHER READING ...

LIFE OF THE TRAIL 2

Historic Hikes in Northern Yoho National Park

Emerson Sanford & Janice Sanford Beck

Life of the Trail 2: Historic Hikes in Northern Yoho National Park follows the trails of fur traders La Gasse and Le Blanc, the Palliser Expedition, Tom Wilson, J.J. McArthur, Professor Jean Habel, Walter Wilcox, C.S. Thompson, David Thompson, Jimmy Simpson and Jack Brewster. Along the way, the reader will journey past pristine lakes and glaciers that have become legendary throughout the world, discovering the stories behind routes through the mountain towns of Lake Louise and Field; over Howse, Amiskwi, Bow and Burgess passes; and along Yoho, Emerald and Castleguard rivers.

ISBN 978-1-897522-00-4

Colour Photos, Maps

$26.95, Softcover

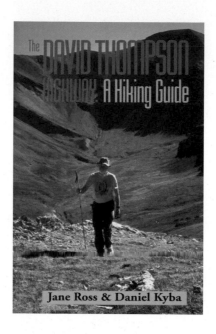

THE DAVID THOMPSON HIGHWAY
A Hiking Guide

Jane Ross & Daniel Kyba

This guide describes accessible hikes along Alberta's David Thompson Highway between Nordegg and Banff National Park. All 69 hikes start from the highway and range from walks of two hours to three-day journeys.

ISBN 978-0921102-70-0

B/W Photos, Maps

$16.95, Softcover

Hiking Canada's Great Divide Trail

Revised & Updated

Dustin Lynx

Trekking the Continental Divide from the U.S. border to Kakwa Lake is a demanding adventure. In this revised and updated guidebook devoted to Canada's 1,200-kilometre Great Divide Trail (GDT), Dustin Lynx helps hikers piece together the myriad individual routes that form a continuous trail along the Divide. Lynx's indispensable pre-trip planning advice will help long-distance hikers overcome daunting logistical challenges such as resupply, navigation and access.

ISBN 978-1-894765-89-3

B/W Photos, Maps

$24.95, Softcover

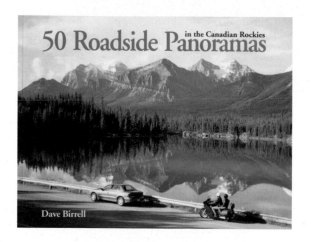

50 Roadside Panoramas in the Canadian Rockies

Dave Birrell

Dave Birrell brings you 50 panoramas taken from highway viewpoints in the Canadian Rockies and the Eastern Slopes between Yellowhead Pass and Waterton. Photographs are accompanied by knowledgeable text, providing you with the fascinating stories behind the names of geographical features: mountains, passes, valleys and lakes.

ISBN 978-0921102-65-6

Illustrated

$24.95, Softcover

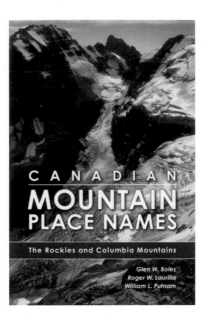

Canadian Mountain Place Names
The Rockies and Columbia Mountains

Glen W. Boles, Roger W. Laurilla, William L. Putnam

This is an entertaining and informative treatise on the toponymy of this increasingly popular alpine region, featuring the names of peaks, rivers, lakes and other geographic landmarks.

ISBN 978-1-894765-79-4
B/W Photos, Line Drawings
$19.95, Softcover

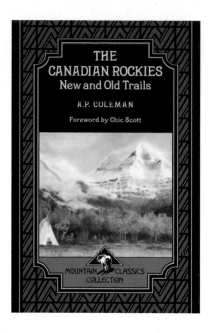

THE CANADIAN ROCKIES: NEW AND OLD TRAILS
Mountain Classics Collection 1

A.P. Coleman
Foreword by Chic Scott

First published in 1911, this book gives modern-day readers a glimpse of the early days of mountaineering in the Canadian West. It paints a sympathetic picture of the rugged men and women who opened the region and of the hardships they endured.

ISBN 978-1894765-76-3

$19.95, Softcover

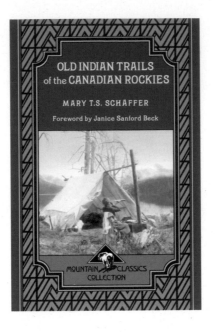

OLD INDIAN TRAILS OF THE CANADIAN ROCKIES
Mountain Classics Collection 2

Mary T.S. Schäffer
Foreword by Janice Sanford Beck

Mary T.S. Schäffer was an avid explorer and one of the first non-Native women to venture into the heart of the Canadian Rocky Mountains, where few women – or men – had gone before. First published in 1911, Old Indian Trails of the Canadian Rockies is Schäffer's story of her adventures in the traditionally male-dominated world of climbing and exploration.

ISBN 978-1-894765-77-0

$19.95 Softcover

IN THE HEART OF THE CANADIAN ROCKIES
Mountain Classics Collection 3

James Outram
Foreword by Chic Scott

Born in 1864 in London, England, James Outram was a Church of England clergyman, mountaineer, author, businessman, militia officer and Orangeman who came to Canada at the turn of the 20th century after travelling and climbing throughout Europe. First published in 1905, In the *Heart of the Canadian Rockies* is Outram's record of his adventures and exploits in the early years of the 20th century among the massive mountains straddling the Alberta/British Columbia boundary.

ISBN 978-1-894765-96-1
$22.95, Softcover

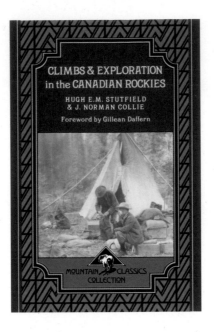

Climbs & Exploration in the Canadian Rockies
Mountain Classics Collection 4

Hugh E.M. Stutfield & J. Norman Collie
Foreword by Gillean Daffern

First published in 1903, *Climbs & Exploration in the Canadian Rockies* details the mountaineering adventures of Hugh Stutfield and J. Norman Collie while the two were together during various explorations in the area north of Lake Louise, Alberta. Between 1898 and 1902, Stutfield and Collie journeyed through the mountain towns, valleys and passes of the Rockies, where Collie completed numerous first ascents and discovered fresh views of Lake Louise and the Columbia Icefields.

ISBN 978-1-897522-06-6

$22.95, Softcover

MOUNT ASSINIBOINE
Images in Art

Jane Lytton Gooch
Preface by Robert Sandford

Mount Assiniboine: Images in Art highlights a century of landscape art inspired by the Mount Assiniboine area of the Canadian Rockies from 1899 to 2006. The main text presents 42 colour plates illustrating a wide variety of styles and media from 23 artists including A.P. Coleman, Carl Rungius, James Simpson, Belmore Browne, Barbara and A.C. Leighton, Catharine and Peter Whyte, W.J. Phillips and A.Y. Jackson.

ISBN 978-1-894765-97-8
B/W & Colour Images
$29.95, Softcover